T0124491

The Very Secret Sex Lives of Medieval Women

The Very Secret Sex Lives of Medieval Women

An Inside Look at Women and Sex in Medieval Times

Rosalie Gilbert

Coral Gables

Published by Mango Publishing Group, a division of Mango Media Inc.

Front cover illustration: Tania Crossingham Illuminations & Fine Art © 2019

Book Cover and Interior Design: Jermaine Lau

For permission requests, please contact the publisher at:
Mango Publishing Group
2850 S Douglas Road, 2nd Floor
Coral Gables, FL 33134 USA
info@mango.bz

For special orders, quantity sales, course adoptions and corporate sales, please email the publisher at sales@mango.bz. For trade and wholesale sales, please contact Ingram Publisher Services at customer.service@ingramcontent.com or +1.800.509.4887.

The Very Secret Sex Lives of Medieval Women: An Inside Look at Women and Sex in Medieval Times

LCCN: 2020933891

BISAC: BIO022000—BIOGRAPHY & AUTOBIOGRAPHY / Women

Printed in the United States of America

Disclaimer

This work of literature contains many herbal recipes, preparations, and advice from medieval manuscripts which you are ill-advised to attempt at home. Seriously. Don't try them. The harm that ensues may be life-threatening and permanent. Death may come to you on swift wings.

I repeat, **Do Not Try These At Home.**

Except if you're trying to lure a unicorn with your virginity.

If you're doing that, feel free to keep up the good work.

For Jenny,

who is changing the roster as we speak.

#sorrynotsorry

Table of Contents

Introduction

Getting Sexy Medieval-Style

We know that Medieval women had sex. We know this. It's a fact. Babies were born. They grew up and had babies of their own and, in order for that to happen, the act of procreation must have occurred. This much we do know, but have you ever wondered what sex was like for the Medieval woman?

Were women slaves to their husbands' every desire? Were they secured safely and jealously in a chastity belt in his absence? Was sex a duty or could it be a pleasure? Did the Medieval woman have any say about her own body and who did or didn't get up close and personal with it at all? Ever? About any of it?

So much more than you might think.

In the modern world, we have the Victorian scholars to thank for many of the grossly misleading ideas about the women who came before us in the Medieval world. Many of the so-called facts that we think we know today can be directly attributed to them. The Victorian era was full of smug people who were quite delighted with their own society and how clever it was and concluded loudly in literature everywhere what an awful, backwards, uncultured, and uncivilised society everyone before their own had been. This flew in the face of historical evidence of Romans, Etruscans, and the Spanish Inquisition. Okay, the Inquisition was uncivilised in the respect that religious mania persecuted humans in brutal and horrendous ways, but the religious and domestic arts and science of the time period were not.

Unfortunately, no one questioned any of these Victorian ideas because—wait for it—contemporary Victorians *also agreed*. There was no kind of peer review process where an enquiring scholar might challenge an history authority or meekly enquire whether things were being blown out of proportion a little and looking into it properly might be a good idea. No. They had ideas about Medieval people, and they stuck to them.

The biggest problem with this is, as Hollywood found its feet and blossomed into a thriving industry, producers read a lot of books and then just ran with what they found there. They cherry-picked their favourite bits. Costumes, customs, and depictions of historical life were gleefully snatched from the pages of Victorian writers, and suddenly, what the world knew to be true about past lives was *their* interpretation of it.

Vikings gained horned helmets. Viking women got those coconut-shaped breast covers. Pointy princess hats called *hennins*, which were popular for a very, *very* short time, became the must-have item for every Medieval woman, regardless of what else she was wearing. Fur rugs were draped over absolutely everything, and castle walls were unpainted stones. Peasants were dressed in clothing which was poorly sewn and ill-fitting, and everyone wore brown. Even the black, rotting teeth we see in movies is inaccurate, not coming until the widespread use of sugar, and is not indicative of general hygiene standards in the Middle Ages.

Likewise, Medieval women suffered at the hands of the Victorian imaginings. Women couldn't read. They had no say about anything and couldn't own property or run businesses. They didn't wear makeup or underpants. And chastity belts were insisted upon. It was really quite unfair.

In fact, Medieval women had tweezers and shaped their eyebrows. They cared about their appearance. Poor women had very little, but because they had little, it was made to last and was less disposable than our cheap chain store clothing of today. Hinting that clothing which was hand spun and handwoven was also poorly made is insulting and incorrect. A woman who had learned to sew from a very early age was extremely good at it by the time she was required to produce clothing for her family.

The intimate lives of Medieval women were as complex and as complicated as ours today, with very little being clear cut and many of the issues relating to sexual relationships having distinctly blurry edges. Women then, as now, loved and lost, hoped and schemed, laughed and cried, were lifted up and cast

down. They were hopeful and lovelorn. Some were chaste and some were lusty. Some had sex thrust unwillingly upon them and had to deal with the consequences. Others made aphrodisiacs and dressed for success.

Sometimes having sex was complicated. Sometimes not having sex was even more so. In spite of the hundreds of years which separate the very secret sex lives of Medieval women and the sex lives of modern women, many similarities remain. Only the actual women have changed. These are true stories of over one hundred actual Medieval women.

Let's go and meet them now.

Chapter 1

How to Know If You're Having It

Unlike today, a Medieval woman's status in society wasn't gauged by her age or by her level of education, profession, or her career successes, but by her sexual status. She was either:

- a virgin (young, unmarried, not allowed to have sex)
- a wife (married, allowed to have sex)
- a widow (ex-married, not allowed to have sex)
- a strumpette (single, having or suspected of having sex)

...and her rights and obligations in society were hugely dependant on this.

An unmarried woman, generally speaking, was a dependant in her father's household and was pretty much nothing more than a marriageable commodity who was to enrich someone else's family in the future. She might have some education and skills, but, on the whole, she was seen as not having found her place in society just yet.

A married woman was accorded respect as a wife and mother, manager of a household, and a person who might also work in her husband's business. She might have a trade. She was the wife of somebody, and everything she did, good or bad, reflected on him.

If a woman wasn't either of those things, she had special circumstances attached to her or she was walking a fine line which was leading to certain doom. Married women who were not faithful to their husbands were liable to find themselves in a

situation ending badly, as adultery was a serious crime. There was a fine line between courtly love and just getting a bit on the side.

Virgins

As far as sex is concerned, if you're young and single, you're undoubtedly a virgin and you're not having sex. At all. Your haystack is unrolled, your rose garden is un-walked in, and your ring is un-speared. Virgins were not only a valuable commodity; their very purity could, according to legend, lure unicorns. Even if actual unicorns were mythical, it can be said that virgins did attract a number of beasts who had a horn where their brain should be.

There were two types of virgins in Medieval society. Both guarded their virginity fiercely, but for very different reasons.

Virgins by Circumstance

These were usually girls and young women who were not yet wed and who, in the fullness of time, would become wives and mothers. Their chastity was critical if they were to make good, and often financially profitable, marriages. The higher the class of the girl, the less likely she be left unchaperoned and the more likely that her future husband and sex partner was to be determined for her. We know that many a young bride-to-be viewed this arrangement with trepidation, and who could blame her?

A young lady who was marrying someone socially important might have her virginity verified by female doctors or religious women before her nuptials proceeded to the signing-of-the-goods-and-chattels stage, but this was absolutely not the usual thing for everyday women. Failure to pass this test guaranteed shame and scandal in the family and the broader community.

Penalties for raping a virgin were extremely severe as a good marriage afterwards was next to impossible.

It simply wouldn't do.

Saint Agnes of Rome

Virgins in a perilous world needed special protection, and Saint Agnes was the go-to saint for virgins of any age. She was known under a few different names, Agnes of Rome, Ines, Ynez, and Ines del Campo, but is usually easy to identify as she is almost always shown with her signature lamb. Although *agnus* is the Latin word for *lamb*, Agnes is a Greek word meaning *pure*, *chaste*, and *sacred*.

St Agnes was born in 291 AD in Rome. For her age, she had rather strong feelings about Christianity and resisted all efforts and bribes to get her to change her mind. Agnes had never wished to marry at all, citing Jesus as her only spouse, even as a pre-teen. There are conflicting accounts of her martyrdom, but most agree that she was around twelve or thirteen when she refused a betrothal to a Roman official's son and was decapitated on January 21, 304 AD.

Her skull is housed today for visiting pilgrims in a side chapel of the Church of Saint Agnes in Agony in Piazza Navona, Rome. It is a monument to those who pray to keep their virginity, which is the exact opposite of the point her parents were trying to make.

The biggest problem with being a virgin in Medieval society is that men absolutely wanted to have sex with you, with little regard for your age, your occupation, or whether or not you'd made a vow to God to remain so. One of the stories in the chronicles of the Congregation of the Apostles in Parma illustrates this clearly.

The Widow's Daughter of Parma

It was the early thirteenth century when a widow's daughter had the misfortune to be home when some itinerant monks came calling. Gherardino Segarello had great plans to be a holy man

and is recorded to have stayed overnight at a certain widow's house for shelter. He noted that she had a virgin daughter and said that God had spoken to him, commanding him to test his chastity by laying naked with the daughter for the night. The mother was not convinced in the least, but Gherardino was not thwarted and quoted bible verses at her from the Gospel of Saint Matthew, stating that men may make themselves eunuchs for the Kingdom of God and that her daughter was in no danger of losing her virginity. She believed him. He lied.

Virgins by Choice

The second kind of virgin was the Virgin-by-Choice. These adult women had consciously made the decision to remain chaste, usually paired with a commitment to God to continue to do so for the foreseeable future. In some cases, this was seen to be admirable, but in other cases, not so much.

Christina of Markyate was one of the latter.

Theodora of Huntingdon a.k.a. Christina of Markyate

Christina was an Anglo-Saxon born in Huntingdon, England around 1096 to 1098. Her birth name was Theodora. Her parents Beatrix and Auti were wealthy merchants and not more religious, especially, than others in their town. As a little girl, Theodora talked to Christ as if he were a real person she could see. When she became a teen, she visited St Alban's Abbey in Hertfordshire where she was so overcome with devoutness that she took a secret vow of chastity right then and there.

At some point, Theodora was visiting her aunt when a visiting bishop got the hots for her and tried to make her his lover. Being a smart girl, Theodora helpfully suggested that she lock the door to guarantee their privacy. The bishop agreed, but she locked him inside the room without her. Needless to say, this did not go down well.

Angry at being spurned, the bishop arranged a marriage for Theodora with a nobleman named Beorhtred.

Theodora's parents agreed to the match, but Theodora refused. Her parents were furious. They tried all the usual things, bewitching her, getting her drunk, pulling her hair, beatings, and threats, but none made any great impression, and Theodora stuck to her guns. In a desperate effort to make the marriage happen, her parents arranged that Beorhtred would have access to her bedroom so that he might enter at night and rape her, thus forcing the marriage.

Things took a disappointing turn for the worse from there.

The next morning, when Theodora's parents came to the room to check how things were moving along, they were aghast to find that Theodora had spent the night telling the disappointed man stories about chaste marriages and other virtuous women.

Unsurprisingly, Beorhtred's friends mocked him mercilessly for failing to get the girl. Not to be deterred, her parents let the determined groom-to-be into her room a second time and hoped for better results. Apparently, Theodora hid behind a tapestry, and Beorhtred couldn't find her, which tells us a little about the kind of guy he was and hints that he was not as determined as he first seemed.

Eventually, Theodora escaped, disguised in men's clothing, and was secreted away with an anchoress at Flamstead. It was here that she changed her name to Christina and devoted the rest of her life to chastity and worship, becoming the head of a community of nuns. She died a virgin in about 1155. Christina 1: Parents 0.

A woman praying.

Helmarshausen Psalter, Noble lady at prayer, Walters Ex Libris. Manuscript W10, folio 6v.

Christina wasn't the only one to take advantage of the shelter that religious houses offered. The best news of all is that those women who wished to live chaste lives in the name of holiness could be married and still enjoy all the perks of being socially elevated as wives. A nun could also avoid getting naked with a husband who didn't rev her engine.

Whilst a vow of chastity was deemed fairly admirable by the general community at large, it could also be quite unfortunate for an eager husband who discovered that his brand-new bride fancied God far more than a romantic interlude with himself. This was particularly unfortunate, because should a husband take his complaint to his priest, he could expect nothing but congratulations for having such an outstandingly pious woman in his life.

Congratulations, indeed.

It was a rather nice loophole for the reluctant wife who had found herself the product of a convenient family union for the purposes of expanding the family estates or an upwardly-mobile social connection. There are not many written records of women who married and remained chaste throughout their entire marriages, but there are a few. These women maintained their virginity despite their disappointed husbands' best efforts.

I imagine it generally went down something a little like this:

Geoffrey is a balding, fat, somewhat rich fifty-year-old and has scored for himself a cute seventeen-year-old bride. The documents have been signed, ceremony performed,

dowry delivered, crowd waiting around the marital bed to verify that intercourse had indeed taken place and all that remains is to bed his bride. Margaret, however, seems quite pensive about the whole situation and is looking for a way out...

Margaret: *My husband, before we retire to bed, I must pray and give thanks to God for this day.*

Geoffrey: *Oh...sure...if you must, my wife, but do hurry. We have some consummating to do!*

Margaret: *Won't be long.*

Ten minutes later

Geoffrey: *Ah...how's it going? You done praying yet? I'm... ah...waiting.*

Margaret: *My husband! My husband! Rejoice! I was praying so hard and, why, it's quite miraculous! The Lord spake to me verily, and bid me love only him with my heart and soul and especially my body and I know you'll be so happy, but I'm overcome with love for our God, and I'm taking a vow of chastity right here and now because of my sudden love for Him and I hereby release you from your marriage debt! Hallelujah! Aren't you so pleased?*

Geoffrey: *That's great Marg... Wait, what?*

Best. Loophole. Ever.

Faking It

If a young woman had been careless with her virginity and her marriage day was drawing near, all was not lost. Methods to make a woman seem like a virgin all over again were available if one knew who to ask. Here we meet a rather remarkable woman by the name of Trotula. She had a lot of great advice about a lot of great things. No, seriously. It's great.

Trotula de Ruggiero

Trotula de Ruggiero was a female medic from the eleventh century who is widely credited for if not writing, then at the very least compiling, the medical health treatise specifically aimed at women, their gynaecological complaints, and other issues which a woman may feel awkward discussing with a man. It was called *De Passionibus Mulierum Curandarum*, or in English, *About Women's Diseases*. Many remedies are for the relief of complaints, rather than actual diseases, but her work was used for an extended period of time and her advice taken in all seriousness. Even the really weird bits.

Restricting It

When it came to faking virginity, Trotula was an ideas woman, and she had two fool-proof ways to trick a husband into thinking he'd married a virgin when, in fact, he hadn't. The first method was to constrict the vagina, so it appeared untouched. She had several ripping recipes to try. I strongly suggest you try exactly none of them at home. Firstly, this one required an extended amount of dedicated administering and quite a bit of spare linen.

> ***A constrictive for the vagina so that they may appear as if they were virgins.***
>
> *Take the whites of eggs, and mix them with water in which pennyroyal and hot herbs of this kind have been cooked, and with a new linen cloth dipped in it, place it in the vagina two or three times a day. And if she urinates at night, put it in again. And note that prior to this, the vagina ought to be washed well with the same warm water with which these things are mixed.*

Well, that's almost helpful, except for the bit about *herbs of this kind*. That's way too vague. It's almost as if she doesn't want to help at all. A woman who is placing anything into her pink bits

A woman with a bottle.

Book of Hours, Marginalia, Walters Ex Libris. Manuscript W87, folio 60v.

or washing them with water steeped in herbs of any kind needs to know exactly what they should be. Guesswork could produce alarming results or be downright fatal. Failure to get a good result could easily be blamed on lack of adequate knowledge of herbology, which doesn't help the bride-to-be in the least.

For the woman of simple means with no one to ask about what kind of specific herbs she needed for the first recipe, Trotula had another nifty DIY which was more explicit, required very few resources and little preparation, and could be made in a reasonable time frame should the wedding be impending sooner than planned.

> *Likewise take the powder of natron or blackberry and put it in; it constricts marvellously.*

Natron is a mineral salt which is found in lake beds. It might be available in a city or town, but not so much in a village nowhere near a lake. Whilst a woman who was low on the socio-economic scale was unlikely to have natron already hanging around the kitchen, she potentially had access to free blackberries growing in the garden. Again, specific recipe directions are lacking, and it's not clear which part of the blackberry is to be powdered. Leaves? Stem? Dried fruit? So many variables. No wonder these things often didn't work.

For the woman who needed to appear virginal and who also had access to a variety of exotic materials, another recipe

which required far less guesswork, but far more financial outlay was this:

> *In another fashion, take oak apples, roses, sumac, great plantain, comfrey, Armenian bole, alum and fuller's earth of each one ounce. Let them be cooked in rainwater and with this water let the genitals be fomented.*

If one wasn't restricted adequately, at least the bole would give the lower lips an attractive rosy glow, the roses would make them smell nice, and the comfrey and the clay of the fuller's earth would be soothing to the potential unpleasantness of the alum. One might just have to fake it after all.

Providing a Bleed

If restricting the vagina either didn't work or didn't restrict it enough, the second of the Trotula-approved methods could be attempted. Her second method was to provide the bleed which was expected of a virgin the first time she had intercourse. She advised this should be done by attaching leeches to the bride's labium one night before she is to be married. Care was advised not to let the leeches go in too far, but I'm not sure how one goes about that. Put them on a little leash? The blood from the leeches is then...

> *...converted into a little clot...the man will be deceived by the effusion of blood.*

This would prove the necessary innocence of his bride and all would be well. Explaining the jar of leeches the next morning might not be quite so easy. Removal of a wayward leech, even more so. Trotula doesn't mention whether to remove the leeches before coitus, but one assumes so. Having a leech detach from the lady and attach itself onto the penis is likely to raise uncomfortable questions all round.

A much more alarming recipe that seems almost guaranteed to provoke bleeding was to make a pomade of ground glass and dye and insert it into the vagina pre-coitus. I feel the dye is completely not needed in this case, as pasting some ground glass into your most vulnerable part seems quite likely to provide all the blood a woman might need. The trick would be getting it to stop. I don't even want to think about what this might do to the unfortunate penis of the husband.

Trotula wrote that this was favoured by prostitutes who wishes to appear virginal, but that it was ill-advised. You don't say.

The Perils of Virginhood

Being a virgin was not just as simple as Just Saying No. The youthful virgin had only to be concerned with whom she was paired up with as a future husband and whether he was old and unattractive or someone she might come to love. She was usually chaperoned or in the care of an adult as she learned how to manage a household and master domestic tasks.

The older virgin had to guard her maidenhead from rape, which could be either an act of random attack, but sometimes was an effort to gain a marriage. Once a woman had been carnally known, chances are, the man responsible was liable to marry her. This might secure a reluctant bride who had already turned down an offer of marriage or, in some cases, force parents who felt the prospective groom was unsuitable to agree to a union.

Historiated initial C with a ravished virgin marrying her assailant. Walters Ex Libris. Manuscript W133, folio 310r.

It was not entirely unheard of for a woman to stage her abduction and rape with her intended husband. The parents would have no choice but to agree to a marriage under those circumstances once she was "spoilt." I am incredibly thankful that neither of these are

widespread attitudes we share today. Being ruined or spoilt once one is no longer a virgin is beyond ridiculous. Being forced to marry a man who raped you? Even more so.

Worse than either of those things was the belief that the older virgin may have urgings. She might become lustful. It was a well-known fact that women were more lustful than men, so this was, apparently, an actual concern. One could even tell if a woman was longing for sex just by checking out her urine.

Monkey with a Urine Flask. Marginalia from The Macclesfield Psalter. East Anglia, probably Norwich, England c. 1330–1340 MS1-2005. Getty Images.

According to *Here begins The Seeing Of Urines,* an immensely helpful writing on how urine looks, smells, and tastes, a woman who was feeling amorous could be diagnosed by the kind of urine she was passing at the time. It tells us:

> *Urine of a woman coloured as bright gold betokens talent or desirous of the company of men.*

Which is a bit broad, I must say. Talented or lusty? Both? You decide.

Going It Alone

Happily, many medical treatises offered delightfully optimistic help about how to quench improper longings of the flesh that a weak female might have. For example, the *Paenitentiale Theodori,* or the *Penitential of Theodore*, written by the Archbishop Theodore of Canterbury in 700 AD, is only a little bit annoyed with the man who takes things into his own hands. Masturbation? Penance of a mere three weeks. For the women who do likewise:

> *If a woman...practices solitary vice, she shall do penance for the same period.*

On this topic, men and women are on an equal footing in regard to deeds and punishments. Ladies who liked to touch was of concern not only to men of the cloth, but to other women also.

Here we first meet Hildegard von Bingen, a young German woman who was handed over to an anchoress for the express purpose of educational opportunities at the tender age of eight. One hopes she was a virgin at the time.

Hildegard von Bingen of Bockelheim

Hildegard was born in 1098 in Germany and became a learned healer, musician, artist, poet, saint, visionary, and abbess. Her books *Physica* and *Holistic Healing* dealt with things of nature, ailments and what to do about them, and was widely circulated in her lifetime in the twelfth century and continued to be copied and distributed throughout the entire medieval period. She had helpful recommendations for every occasion, including for the woman who was hopelessly inflicted with lust. Mandrake was the answer.

> *If a woman suffers the same ardour in her body, she should put a piece of male mandrake root between her breast and belly button...for three days and three nights. Later,*

divide it into two parts, and keep one part tied each side of the groin for three days and three nights... But she should pulverise the right hand of it and add a bit of camphor. After eating it her ardour will be extinguished.

Male Mandrake, Hortus Sanitatis: mandrake.

Credit: Wellcome Collection. CC BY.

If one isn't too sure how to tell a male mandrake from a female, it's easy. Male mandrakes have leaves similar to the beet whereas female mandrakes have leaves like lettuce and produce fruit like plums, according to Isidore of Seville. To attempt this kind of recipe without the correct type of mandrake was sure to end in a disappointingly poor result. Call me sceptical, but I'm not sure that tying things to the groin is a really great way to avoid thinking about sex.

Women who weren't virgins or were recently virgins were, it was hoped, legitimate wives and mothers of soon-to-be mothers.

Wives and Mothers

Generally speaking, it was the social norm for girls to grow up, mature, wed, and become mothers. Women were lustier than men, and marriage was the socially-approved outlet for sexual activity. Heaven forbid that a female might be lusty by herself. She definitely needed a husband to share all that lust with.

Clergymen were often simultaneously in favour and not in favour of marriage. It was needed, sure, but it was likely to be the cause of some deep regret. Thomas of Chobham was born a little later than Hildegard von Bingen in 1160, but he, too, was a man of the cloth and wrote extensively on a number of items relating to men and women and their intimate relationships. He became sub-dean of Salisbury, but in his earlier days, he started off with a sweet and almost tender view of marriage.

> *In contracting marriage a man gives a woman his body, and she hers; apart from the soul, nothing under the sky is more precious.*

It's quite romantic. This was countered by his thoughts of chastisement and sex, but we'll get to that later. For now, Thomas appears to be of no particular bias and wants happiness for both sexes. Later, he wrote extensively about sinning in his *Confessor's Manual*. Another Thomas, the Dominican preacher Thomas of Cantimpré, who was born in 1201 in Belgium before becoming a Flemish Roman Catholic, has this to say in his book on vices and virtues:

> *It is right for those folk thus to have consolation of a moderate joy, who have joined together in the laborious life of matrimony. For according to the vulgar proverb, that man is worthy to have a little bell hung on a golden chain around his neck, who hath not repented of taking a wife before the year is out.*

Thanks a bunch, Thomas. Moderate joy, indeed. One feels that he is softening the blow of how awful the future of a man who has decided to marry is by using a bell on a golden chain to depict the slavery of having a wife. It's better than a ball and chain at any rate.

Both Roman Canon and civil law gave the marriageable age for a girl at twelve, which roughly coincided with the onset of puberty.

Puberty, being subject to the individual, sometimes occurred earlier or later, of course. Boys were marriageable at fourteen years of age.

Historiated initial "C" showing a woman seeking an annulment after being deceived into marrying a man in the guise of her suitor.
Gratian's Decretum, Walters Manuscript W.133, fol. 263r.

Most marriages were arranged by the parents and very hard to escape once entered into. Parents often used strong arm tactics to encourage reluctant daughters to consent to wed. Rarely do women secure annulments for a bad match, but it became a complaint the courts heard more and more often. Cases might be annulled where trickery was involved, consanguinity, impotence, or severe brutality, although husbands were encouraged to chastise their wives moderately.

Catherine McKesky of Ireland

One fifteenth-century Irish wife who hadn't wished to marry in the first place, Catherine McKesky, desperately appealed for an annulment from her husband, John Cusake. In 1436, she brought witnesses to speak for her who testified that she had been forced

into betrothal by severe and repeated beatings from her family and had made her despair known loudly all throughout her engagement. Her consent at the altar to wed was given freely as much as anyone who was literally likely to be beaten to death for refusing. The marriage was annulled, in this case.

Nothing secured a marriage like producing an heir—or several—and it had the double bonus of security in a woman's old age. A married woman held a significantly higher place in society than an unmarried one. She had assets and responsibilities. She was someone. The marital debt meant that marriage and sex went hand in hand. Cardinal Hostiensis explains this from his writings in the thirteenth century.

> *Husbands have a moral obligation to keep their wives sexually satisfied, lest they be tempted to stray to other beds.*

Because husbands never stray from the marital bed, right?

Marriages might be performed almost anywhere and everywhere until the church decided that this just wasn't good enough and stepped in to set up a heap of rules about this, too. There were very few rules about *when* a person couldn't get married—the weeks of Advent and Lent being the two most important ones.

There were a large number of rules about *who* a person could marry, restrictions with being too closely related featuring heavily in most of them. In some cases, if a marriage wasn't working out the way a couple hoped, one of the partners could suddenly and conveniently remember that they were too closely related through marriage or blood and that, unfortunately, the marriage should be annulled. Court cases show that this worked on a number of occasions, although it was conveniently overlooked at the time of marriage.

Joanna of Poitou and Eleanor of Poitou

Lower-class and working-class women were married off at a slightly later age than noble girls who were targeted for marriage as soon as they were physically able to produce babies, or earlier. For some, this was at quite a tender age.

In the thirteenth century, little Joanna was engaged at the age of four as part of a peace settlement between King John and a family of Poitou. Her younger sister, who later became the Countess Eleanor, had been married at only nine years of age to the English Earl William Marshall the Younger.

Mary de Bohun of England

It was sadly also the case of twelve-year-old Mary de Bohun who was born in 1369. Married to the future King Henry IV in 1380, she died whilst pregnant with her sixth child at her home in Peterborough Castle in 1394, horrifyingly, at twenty-two. Six pregnancies by the age of twenty-two!

Take a moment to reflect on the twenty-two-year-old young women in your society right now and consider how well they'd be doing with their sixth pregnancy. Many aren't even married, in serious relationships, or on their first pregnancy. Six is a number which is hard to reconcile.

Whilst a marriage itself wasn't performed until twelve, betrothal was permitted by the church at the age of seven. This hinged on the agreement of both parties, but most children do what their parents assure is best for them, so many betrothals went ahead without impediment. We have no records of conversations between mothers and daughters about this, but parents everywhere know that getting a seven-year-old girl to do what you want is just a matter of pushing the right buttons.

Margery is six and three quarters. Her parents have secured a potentially profitable marriage for her with the son of a neighbour. Margery herself is the heir to huge tracts of land

and both parents are keen to secure the transaction. The dowry is set. The marriage date is set. All that remains is to get her to willingly agree.

Mother: *Oh Margery! Exciting news! A husband has been found for you!*

Margery: *I like my new shoes! Do you like my new shoes?*

Mother: *They're very nice, Margery. But a husband! How exciting!*

Margery: *I think these are my favourite shoes ever.*

Mother: *Yes, darling child. Let me tell you about your husband to be!*

Margery: *The only thing I like more than these shoes is my red shoes with the buckles.*

Mother: *Margery! Pay attention. Let me tell you about your Geoffrey, your future husband.*

Margery: *(Pausing) Can I have a pony?*

Mother: *Geoffrey is a nice boy and he's so grown up! He's fifteen!*

Margery: *Anne has a pony. Can I have a pony?*

Mother: *If you marry Geoffrey, you can have all the ponies you want.*

Margery: *Really? As many as I want?*

Mother: *Geoffrey will buy you everything you want! Won't that be lovely?*

Margery: *I want a pony. And some more shoes like these ones.*

Mother: *So, you'll marry Geoffrey like a good girl?*

Margery: *Okay...pause... But only if he brings me a pony nicer than Anne's.*

Although twelve seems extremely young for a young woman to make her mind up about a legally binding situation like marriage

and understand all its physical implications, young women did willingly and knowingly enter into such arrangements. A marriage performed unwillingly or too early allowed it to be negated. We know this from court records where matrimonial ages, usually of the bride, were questioned. If both parties were of-age and consented, all was well. Everything had to be above board and the promises made in the correct manner.

Agnes of York

Sometimes, marriage came quite swiftly if a couple looked like they were in danger of getting carnal and were interrupted by a third party. Vows needed to be said properly in order for them to be considered valid. "I *will* take you" definitely does not mean "I *do* take you right now," an oversight Alice was not going to make when she walked in on Robert and Agnes who were secluded, naked, and potentially up to no good in her own house. The Act Book from the Dean and Chapter of York gives us her hasty intervention:

> *1381. On Monday night before the feast of the Ascention last she came to a certain high room located inside the dwellinghouse of the said witness where she found, as she says, Robert and Agnes lying alone together in one bed.*
>
> *The witness asked Robert, "What are you doing here, Robert?"*
>
> *To this Robert replied, "I'm here already."*
>
> *The witness said to him. "Take Agnes by the hand in order to betroth her."*
>
> *Robert said to the witness, "I beg you wait until the morning."*
>
> *The witness said, "By God, no. You'll do it now."*
>
> *Then Robert took Agnes by the hand and said, "I will take you as my wife."*

The witness said to him, "You will speak in this manner: I take you Agnes to my wife and to this I plight you my troth," and Robert, thus instructed by the witness, took Agnes by the right hand and contracted with her using the words just recited, viz. "Here I take you etc."

Asked how Agnes replied to Robert, she said that Agnes replied to him that she considered herself satisfied. She did not depose further save that she went away and left them alone.

It seems that Robert potentially had ideas about contesting whether he had actually promised anything at all by saying that he *would* take her for his wife in the morning and leaving it all very open-ended. Alice clearly saw right through him and insisted that he say the words properly and make a legally binding contract of engagement. Right. This. Instant.

Being of Age

Being old enough to consent to a marriage was a whole other minefield to be navigated. Record keeping was sketchy at times and sometimes the exact age of the bride was called into question.

One way out of a marriage was simply to say that the bride was not of age and therefore the marriage wasn't binding. Usually this is the case of the groom attempting to escape a marriage, but in one case that we know of, we see a young but determined bride attempting to gather enough witnesses to uphold her marriage.

Alice de Rouclif of York

In November 1385, an entirely different Alice found herself featured in a lengthy court case where she argued adamantly that she was truly married and wanted the marriage to be upheld. The case seemed to hinge on whether she was old enough for

the marriage to be valid and whether or not the marriage was consummated and was therefore proper and binding.

At the time of her alleged marriage, she was under the care of her guardian, Gervase, who may or may not have also been her father. The debate over her age raged over many pages, recorded by the court in York. Witnesses were called to also give evidence about the age of the child bride and explain how they were certain that their account was true and their memories not faulty.

Quite often, regardless of facts, the court got side-tracked looking at the character of the witnesses and whether they were wealthy. Witnesses of independent means and substantial incomes were clearly more reliable and had better memories than poor ones. When looking at the credibility of the witnesses, it was noted that these things were important enough to write down:

> *Alice Sharpe of Rawcliffe, widow, a tenant of Sir Brian de Rouclif, knight, having goods to the value of forty shillings.*
>
> *Alice, wife of William de Tange, of Rawcliffe, tenant of Sir Brian de Rouclif having goods to the value of one mark.*
>
> *Beatrix, wife of John Milner of Clifton, whose goods are worth nine marks.*
>
> *Agnes the Ald, living in Clifton, is not a tenant of Sir Brian de Rouclif, having goods to the value of twenty-two shillings as she says.*
>
> *Joan Symkin, Woman of Rawcliffe, having almost nothing in goods save her clothing for body and bed, and a small brass pot, tenant of Sir Brian de Rouclif.*
>
> *Adam Gaynes, living in St. Marygate in the suburbs of York, deposes that he knew Alice's witnesses for ten years and that they are all poor. He knew John's witnesses for twenty years. They are wealthier than Alice's witnesses.*
>
> *John de Killom of Clifton, knew all the witnesses named for sixteen years. All are of sufficient wealth.*

No prizes for guessing whose word we are taking. Dozens of women like the ones mentioned above who all support each other's claims about the relationship, or one guy who *wasn't even there* and is only a character witness to the *other* witnesses who were involved with the case? Adam isn't even a witness himself, but he knows which side his bread is buttered on, it seems. Rich people have the butter.

In relation to Alice de Rouclif, the witnesses are described as being questioned of her age. This directly relates to the marriage's validity. If Alice was not old enough to make a contract, John could call the whole thing off, regardless of what had happened since, and whether or not he had known her in the biblical sense. In many testimonies, she was eleven at the age of betrothal, but fully twelve at the time of marriage:

> *Concerning her age, Witness Ellen de Rouclif, widow of Elias de Rouclif… She says that she knows well that, before Saturday before the first Sunday in Passiontide next, Alice will be thirteen years and not before. She knows this, as she says, by the fact that this witness gave birth to a daughter, Katherine by name, on the eve of the Feast of the Purification of the Blessed Mary thirteen years ago next, and on the Saturday before the first Sunday in Passiontide following the feast of the Purification, Ellen, the then wife of Gervase de Rouclif, gave birth to the Alice in question. She was not then present at the birth, as she says, but she saw Ellen, Alice's mother, pregnant with her shortly before.*

In other words, the witness Ellen knew that Alice was born then because she had also given birth almost at the same time. She had kept a remembrance of when her daughter Katherine was born, and therefore knew when Alice was.

This manner of remembering a birth in association with another personal event or church occasion was very well utilised in Medieval society. A certain day of the week or month might

be hard to determine, but the church kept note of its feasts and holidays and it was relatively easy to know if something happened a few days before or after. Another way to encourage potential future witnesses' remembering was to give a gift on the day of the birth which was unlikely to be forgotten by the person who received it.

The court records go on extensively about Alice's age and whether she was old enough to marry in the first place before moving on to whether the marriage was consummated and, therefore, a real and binding one. Again, pages of witnesses presented their cases, but none more determinedly than Alice and her family who were keen for the marriage to be upheld. An abbot, who had been confided in by one Joan, deposes:

> *Concerning the marriage being consumed and therefore a real marriage, Dom William Marrays, abbot of St Mary's at York, admitted, sworn, and asked on the aforesaid articles…he says that after the contract of marriage John and Alice ratified this contract of marriage and spousals and lay together alone and naked. This he knows from the relation of both parties, viz, John and Alice, and from a certain Joan Rolleston, who was at that time, Alice's companion in bed and lay in the same room as them, that Alice was present on the night immediately following the feast of St James the Apostle last, and then John knew Alice carnally, as Alice told this witness after Easter last in the fields of Grimston and elsewhere, and Joan also told this witness that she saw John and Alice lying in the same bed together and heard a noise from them like they were making love together, and how two or three times Alice silently complained at the force on account of John's labour as if she had been hurt then as a result of this labour.*

It seems that there was quite a bit of evidence for the match being consummated, but in the very end, it seems uncertain what the outcome of the case was. Other court cases regarding legalities of marriage have elements similar to this one of John and Alice.

Child Marriage

Most of the marriages we know most of are those of royal or noble brides or those who strenuously opposed the match in the first place and petitioned against it loudly and publicly. A well-known example of child marriage is the case of little, but quite well-off Margaret Beaufort.

Margaret Beaufort of Bedfordshire

Margaret Beaufort was born either in the May of 1441 or 1443 in England and was married several times, which says something of her background and her saleability as a bride. In 1450, after her father had passed away and she entered the care of the Duke of Suffolk, William de la Pole, her first marriage to John Pole was arranged.

It was all rather convenient that William's son John happened to be single and looking for a wife. Little Margaret was all of about seven years old and had no say in the matter whatsoever. Happily, her husband was also aged seven and had no say in it either, so at least things were on a bit of an even footing. He wasn't so much looking for a wife either. That was his dad's idea entirely. Other records say she was no older than three years old at the time of her first wedding. Three years later, the marriage was annulled. Neither husband nor wife had consummated the marriage, so it was a relatively simple matter to escape from it.

A further two years later, when Margaret was twelve and of the ability to consent to a marriage herself, she was married to the twenty-four year old Edmund Tudor. Whilst he would have looked like everything a girl could look for in a husband, how he felt about marrying a mere girl of twelve isn't noted. Shortly after the nuptials, war broke out and Edmund died of the plague. Margaret was all of thirteen, a widow, and seven months

pregnant. She was extremely young at the time she gave birth, and Margaret did not give birth again. There is every chance that the birth was complicated, and she suffered damage. This did not, however, seem to make her a less attractive target for remarriage.

Her third marriage to Sir Henry Stafford was annulled because she was too closely related to her husband, who was her second cousin, although that didn't seem to be an issue at the time of marriage when her wealth encouraged the clergy to look the other way. By the age of twenty-eight, she was a widow once again. Still a saleable asset, Margaret was married off again for a fourth time to Thomas Stanley.

Eventually, during her fourth marriage, she took a vow of chastity and lived the remainder of her life avoiding sex altogether. She is best remembered for being the mother of King Henry VII and paternal grandmother of King Henry VIII of England. She was first and foremost a woman, a daughter, a wife, a mother, and a grandmother.

Sex was extremely hard to avoid when married, as the marital debt meant that a husband or wife had every right to ask his spouse for it and a refusal often caused offence. The phrase "won't take no for an answer" usually applied here, even for young women at the age of twelve. Still, there was more than one way to get around this, as we shall see a bit later on.

Widowhood

Widows and chastity went hand in hand. If a woman was a widow, then she certainly wasn't having sex. The rest of the village or town got a bit judgy about that sort of thing, and having a good reputation was a huge consideration which was not lightly abandoned. Besides, a widow had other, more important things going on in their lives, like unsuitable yet hopeful suitors, dealing with their children and assets, and making a living to tend to.

As we know, widows who were well off tended to be targeted for remarriage as, obviously, women shouldn't be left to their own devices, unchaperoned and under the control of no man. Besides, a lot of them had substantial assets which might be better utilised when annexed into some interested man's portfolio.

Pipe Roll Widows

For the woman who wasn't actually looking for another husband, it was often problematic to escape marriage. In the early Medieval days of 1130 England, wealthy widows and orphans were registered on the Exchequer Pipe Rolls with the king who could bestow them as he saw fit, which was all about securing alliances and less about personal happiness and providing a caring environment for the woman herself. Young heiresses were also viewed as tradable property and less as actual humans.

It was possible for a woman to opt out of the register and remain single if she had the funds to do so, however. This sounds like an awful but doable trade-off, but the catch was that usually the buy-out price was so high that most of the women's goods were required to be sold, leaving her poor and in need of a husband to provide for her. It was a brilliant catch-22.

Lucia Thoroldsdottir of Lincoln

Lucia was born in May in 1074 and was a lady not so easily deterred. She was an heiress and a woman of means and determination. Her life mirrored the lives of many other women in her era: a woman who grew up and married, gained a title and added to her riches, and was remarried when her husband died. The pattern of her life had already been repeated three times when she found herself proposing to escape a fourth.

Eleventh-century England offered the opportunity to stay single if the price was right. For a woman like Lucia, the right price was high. Not to be deterred, Lucia raised the funds required and bought her way to freedom. Her offered price was a staggering

500 marks, which was enormous by twelfth-century standards, but even this was only to give her a grace period of five years. Lucia added a further 100 marks to be able to do justice in her own court amongst her own men, although what that fully entailed is a little blurry.

Somewhere along the line, she became the Countess of Chester and is better known to many historians as Lucy of Bolingbroke.

Widow Gybscott of Lincoln and Widow Coll of Oxford

Whilst widows had their good name to protect, they were occasionally noted in the law courts for unseemly behaviour. Many cases seem trivial by today's standards. Being prosecuted for gossiping appears on the surface as an over-reaction; however, it must be remembered that a good name was important and slander might ruin a woman. It still comes across as being a bit childish to take someone to court over what is essentially name-calling.

One entry from the diocese of Lincoln, in England, reads like this:

> *Widow Gybscott is a common defamer of her neighbours.*

...which seems no different from the gossipy old women in communities everywhere. Widow Gybscott was obviously not the only one who liked to point the finger. Two women named Agnes Horton and Joan Whitescale had no great love for each other and were both summoned to court for name-calling, which must have been getting out of hand.

Agnes Horton of Brill and Joan Whitescale of Brill

In defamation suits of 1505 from *The Courts of the Archdeaconry of Buckingham* records we find Agnes and Joan both called in on charges of disturbing the peace with name-calling.

> *1505. Agnes Horton of the parish of Brill and Joan Whitescale of Brill. Summoned ex officio reputed as common scolds calling each other "Thou art a strong whore" and vice versa.*

Clearly, there was no real love between these two women and one can only imagine the circumstances which led to a court appearance. There is no indication of whether they were married or what the circumstances were. Were their husbands business rivals? Were they both single and had their eyes on the same man? Was one of them an actual whore and the other calling her out for it? Did they dress a little too casually and just look like they were trying to catch the eyes of any and all men they met?

Who knew? It sounds like there is definitely a back story there which is grounded in their personal interactions with each other. Name-calling rarely starts for no reason at all.

Widow Coll of Oxford

In another rare case, we see a widow who has been extremely charitable in taking in unmarried, pregnant women. Instead of it being seen as a worthy and loving thing to do, it reached the court in the form of a complaint. Her case from St Peter-le-Bailey, Oxford states emphatically:

> *Widow Coll stakes receives pregnant women in her home in which they are cared for.*

Well, hooray for the widow, who seems far more humanitarian than most. It is awful that a woman who is a widow had the inner strength to offer refuge when other women found themselves in the distressing situation of being pregnant. They had no one to turn to and not only got complained about, but taken to a court of law.

Surely caring for the less fortunate was an act of charity? How she pleaded and what the outcome was, we are not told. No

punishment or fine is noted, so perhaps she was let off with a warning.

Vowess or nun was always an option for the reluctant lady.

Nun. Book of Hours, Marginalia, Walters Ex Libris. Manuscript W.87, folio 102v.

If a woman was a widow, she also had the option of becoming a vowess, which meant she promised in all seriousness to keep herself physically chaste and make a promise to God before witnesses. She need not be a nun or enter a convent to do this. It was achieved by taking a public vow of chastity and was a relatively simple process. All a woman needed was a bishop, a ring, a mantle, and a deceased husband.

The bishop oversaw the ceremony, of course, and blessed the ring the widow was to wear. It was assumed that the clothes of a widow would be modest and demure, so no special instructions were given on dress. Married or mature women in most places wore veils and wimples as part of their usual dress and continued to do so as vowesses.

Margaret Beaufort took this step, unusually, whilst her fourth husband was still alive and re-confirmed her vow at his deathbed. She'd been married a few times already as an extremely eligible bride with great political connections and huge tracts of land, and perhaps just wanted to get in early and emphatically state that she planned to give the whole thing a pass from then on. I don't blame her in the least.

Nuns, Vowesses, and Born-Again Virgins

Virgins who had an actual religious vocation could enter a church-approved convent, nunnery, or similar establishment and stay there, safe from the outside world and its possible husbands. Holy women enjoyed the same social standing in society as virgins did. One might think that, as they were unmarried, they might be held in less regard than married women, but this was not the case. Nuns were, for all intents and purposes, married in a spiritual way, which was seen as real as a fleshly one. They were under the domain of no mortal man, rather, a heavenly one: God. He was, in all essence, their heavenly bridegroom, and their vows to him were as serious and as binding.

In reality, nuns were under the rule of a head lady called an abbess who oversaw the running of the nunnery and saw to the spiritual well-being of the ladies who lived there. The abbess demanded complete chasteness at all times with varying degrees of success.

If a woman had joined a religious order later in life and had at one time been a sexually active wife, she was no longer an actual virgin, but might be considered a virgin, reborn as a bride of Christ. Using this fantastic logic, holy women usually fell into the same category as unmarried, and therefore chaste, virginal women. I'd like to see that brought back.

Born-again virgins. Sign me up.

Prostitutes

It should come as absolutely no surprise to anyone that the group of women having the most sex were prostitutes. We'll be taking a long, hard look at them later.

I know many men did.

Loose Women and Unmarried Mothers

In spite of the fairly rigid social construct of who was expected to be having sex and who was not, illicit sex before marriage did happen. No, really. An unmarried woman who was not a virgin—either because she was a mistress, prostitute, or woman of questionable morals—faced not only the malicious gossip of the ladies in the village, but the outright scorn of women everywhere for her shocking life decisions.

She was deciding to risk pregnancy outside of wedlock. It was scandalous. It was irresponsible.

Pregnancy out of wedlock was calamity. The child would certainly not get the inheritance otherwise owing a child of a legal marriage when it came of age. No inheritance. No assets. No dowry. No titles. A bastard child of a regular person was entitled to exactly nothing and because of that, a sexually active unmarried woman was scorned. Not quite so much for the sexual incontinence, which was deemed terrible in itself, but for her appalling lack of effort to secure her potential child's assets by having sexual relations before tying the knot. As a direct result, she herself would have no security in her old age, and that was unforgivable.

If a woman became pregnant out of wedlock, she had only a few options. Her three best choices were to marry and make it legal, to give the child to either a person or a religious institution as a foundling, or to hide her shame by secretly disposing of it.

Foundlings

The practice of leaving an unwanted baby with a church was known as *oblation*. The first specific hospitals built to receive abandoned babies were established in Italy early in the thirteenth century, but churches had been suffering the little children to come unto them almost since there were churches built.

In some cases, a woman might be extremely fortunate to have her babe supported by the father in the form of finances or housing. He may not marry her, but at least there was a roof over their heads, food on the table, and the child did not want for the necessities of life. Furthermore, the child might be educated and a marriage partner found.

Agnes Walles of Hauxley

One particularly virile dad, the rector of Shepshed, supported at least one of his offspring, but appeared to have sired many others, of whom we know very little. The church court in Lincoln, England only states:

> *1519. John Asterley confessed that he had made Agnes Walles, unmarried, pregnant and that she had given birth to a girl child at Hauxley before Christmas. He had supported the child there from his tithes. He also confessed that had made pregnant Margaret Swynerton, unmarried, and had had three children by her. Margaret is now dead. He also had another child by one Joan Chadwyk, now married, then single. Joan lives at Dunstable... John does not know where Agnes lives now. Because of he confessed these things...the vicar general ordered that from henceforth no other woman should serve in his home and that he should live continently.*

Five children and he married none of the mothers! John was yet another man of the cloth spreading the love of the Lord in a very personal and intimate way with his housekeepers. He might like to consider a valet in the future, or perhaps, do his own dusting and dishes. Yes. That might be best for everyone all round.

Any new mother who was less fortunate than Agnes had even fewer options, as those for unmarried mothers go. If she couldn't afford to keep the baby or it was not practical to work and raise it, she had only a couple of choices remaining.

Abandonment

Should a woman fall pregnant with an unwanted baby, she could leave it with someone else, expose it to the elements, or abandon it. This was not murder by actual death, as the child was alive at the time of abandonment and might always be found by someone else and raised. Of course, it was more likely to be found by wild animals and killed.

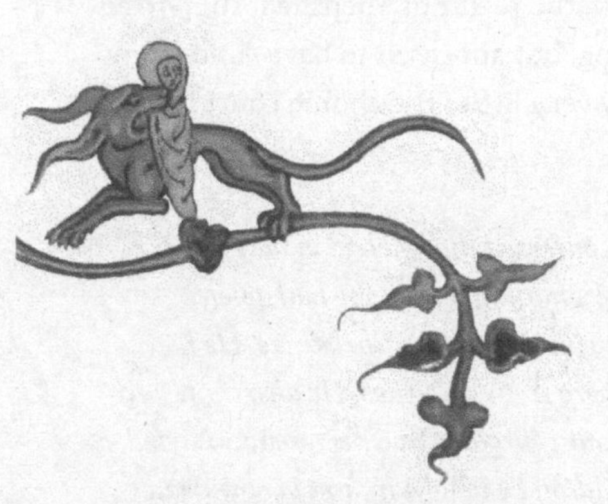

A baby taken by a wild animal.

Marginalia from an incomplete* Book of Hours, *Walters Ex Libris. Manuscript W.87, folio 34r.

More than one record from Medieval English courts survive which show this practice being carried out, although the state and emotions of the mother are rarely told.

Baby Leeke's Mother of Surfleet

The sad case of an unmarried mother comes to us from the courts in 1519, from the Visitations in the Diocese of Lincoln. We don't know how old the mother was or what the circumstance of the pregnancy was, only that the infant was not able to be raised by his mother. The records show:

> *Surfleet. A baby boy was turned away at the door of Thomas Leeke, but his mother claimed that Thomas Leeke was the father of this baby. Thomas, however, denied this and so the baby was taken away to different places, ill treated and died.*

It seems that the baby was not left in the care of the mother, if it was taken away. We don't know why. It isn't specified where the baby was taken, either. Foundling hospitals generally didn't ill-treat babies, as far as we know. All we do know is that the baby died through lack of nurturing, and it is pretty certain that the mother got absolutely no trauma support of grief counselling.

Margaret Harburgh of Kesteven

Spare a thought for Margaret who was living in Kesteven and appeared before the authorities at Sutton in the Marsh, who had a much worse time of it than baby Leeke's mother as the records from the same visiting diocese show:

> *1519. Sutton in the Marsh. Sir John Wymark, lately chaplain there, made Margaret Harburgh pregnant and... [record damaged]...she gave birth. The same Sir John threw the baby in the sea and so killed it. She now lives in Kesteven.*

Why we need to know where the unhappy Margaret now resides, I don't know. Sir John seems to have been relieved of his post as chaplain, which is probably for the best for all concerned, but he appears to have had possession of the child at some point. One assumes that Sir John and Margaret were not standing at the seaside at the time of child delivery and that she had given him the baby, which he had accepted before taking it to the sea and ending its life. The sense of betrayal she must have felt by this act is unfathomable.

As a man of God, this is especially awful. There are no further notes relating to John being charged for the death of the baby or his current location.

Alice Mortyn of Blossomville

Other women bypassed the paternal half of the parenting and just left the baby out in the elements to fend for itself. The Courts

of the Archdeaconry of Buckingham in 1497 records that in Newton, Blossomville:

> *Alice Mortyn gave birth to a child in the household of the rector there, but the father of the child is not known and, it is said, immediately after the birth the said Alice hid the child in the bog where the child died for want.*

For starters, I'd be looking a bit suspiciously at the rector if the father is "not known." Quite a few records exist of women who were unmarried and keeping house for priests, rectors, and likewise men when they fell pregnant. Coincidence? I think not.

Alice's age is not mentioned, but you can bet that whatever her age, purposefully taking a new-born into a bog and walking away from it because there were no other acceptable options to her was not an easy decision to make. Again, I'd be looking at the rector as the person behind the idea that this was the sane and sensible thing to do. At least, the child stood the tiniest chance of being discovered and taken in by a passer-by, even if it was unlikely.

Lastly, the more drastic option of what to do with an unplanned and unwanted child was to commit infanticide. Murdering another living, breathing human being was a grave sin, and not entered into lightly. Abandonment, oblation, murder—apart from the moral wrongdoing by the mother herself, any of these options required the assistance of a trusted third party to help birth the baby and therefore risked discovery, if not instantly, then later at a regretful confession.

Infanticide

The practice of physically disposing of an unwanted baby was not unknown in the Middle Ages. Of course, it was penalised harshly. Infanticide was, for the most part, equated with murder, although in one unusual record from a fourteenth-century court case in Europe, it was not.

An Unnamed Woman

An unnamed woman had been arrested whilst trying to drown her new-born child in a river. The case was heard by twenty-four jurors, all of whom were men. They finally concluded that she was not guilty of infanticide, stating:

> *The woman is not to be punished by any means. And this is so because she bore a baby boy and had her own right to him. Thus, she may kill him and make him perish, for everyone is free to do with what is his, or hers, that which he, or she, pleases to do.*

Why the sex of the baby was mentioned in particular is interesting. Would it have made any difference if the baby was a girl? Boys were heirs and more valuable as offspring, so would they not be the ones to keep and girls be the ones it mattered less to drown? It doesn't make sense. Today, the penalty of the crime would focus on the wilful murder itself, regardless of the gender of the babe.

This was in no way the view of the church or of civil England where harsh penalties usually applied.

Alice Ridyng of Eton

Alice Ridyng was an English woman who murdered and disposed of her baby in 1517, having denied her pregnancy the entire time. Hiding a pregnancy to full term without arousing the suspicions of others was not an easy thing to achieve, as we will read:

> *1517. Alice Ridyng, unmarried, the daughter of John Ridyng of Eton in the diocese of Lincoln appeared in person and confessed that she had conceived a boy child by one Thomas Denys, then chaplain to Master Geoffrey Wren, and gave birth to him at her father's home at Eton one Sunday last month and immediately after giving birth, that is within four hours of the birth, killed the child by putting*

> *her hand in the baby's mouth and so suffocated him. After she had killed the child she buried it in a dung heap in her father's orchard.*
>
> *At the time of delivery, she had no midwife and nobody was ever told as such that she was pregnant, but some women of Windsor and Eton has suspected she was pregnant, but Alice always denied this saying that something else was wrong with her belly. On the Tuesday after the delivery of the child, however, the women and honest wives of Windsor and Eton took her and inspected her belly and her breasts by which they knew for certain that she had given birth. She then confessed everything to them and showed them the place where she had put the dead child.*

These court records give us nothing but the bare bones of what happened without any sense of the emotion of the people directly involved in them. This Alice first kept her pregnancy a secret for the entire duration, dealing with possible morning sickness, fatigue, and clothes which would no longer fit or conceal her predicament, and was left to grieve alone.

Before taking this step, one can only imagine what an emotion-charged first four hours Alice had with her new little baby boy after delivering him herself with no assistance from anyone. It appears that giving him to someone else to raise was not an option for her, but neither was just leaving it with a church, saying she had found it somewhere.

We are also not told how old Alice was, but for her to be living at home and unmarried, chances are that she wasn't terribly old. A bold move by the chaplain, to make moves on his employer's daughter rather than a lowly servant girl who was the usual target for this kind of thing.

Elizabeth Nelson of Pollongton

In most cases, the pregnancy was not hidden and a woman with child would be found out and shamed sooner rather than later.

Throwing herself on the mercy of the church was an option, but not a terribly good one.

The church was bound to offer sanctuary from civil law to any person who sought it, but only for forty days. After that, the person was expelled, forcibly if necessary, often into the waiting arms of the law. From the Sanctuary register of Beverley in England, 1511, we find Elizabeth on the run and fast running out of options:

> *12th day of March in the reign of King Henry the Eighth. Elizabeth Nelson of Pollongton in the country of York, spinster, came to the peace of St John of Beverley for felony and murder of her child killed at Hull, and she was admitted and sworn.*

In many cases, persons who sought sanctuary fled under cover of darkness and left the county, if not the country. We have no further record of what happened to Elizabeth when her forty days came to an end, only that she was unmarried, had been pregnant, and was being pursued for the crime of infanticide. If she was traumatised and repentant, she might take the veil and spend the rest of her life praying for forgiveness.

We don't just have records from court rolls to rely on.

Cess Pits and Other Methods of Disposal

Cautionary tales from illuminated manuscripts also warn of illicit liaisons and, in one case, provide illustrated in full colour. Dated at 1327, the *Miracles De Notre Dame* from Hague tells the tale of a woman who had unhappily caught the attention of her uncle and became with child. The left-hand side of the image shows her reluctant embrace, and the right-hand side shows the result: an illegitimate child who is being thrown down into the toilet.

Legend of the woman having three children by her uncle.

The Hague, Koninklijke Bibliotheek, 71 A 24. Folio 176r.

This is an extremely rare picture of an actual toilet, showing an equally rare action. Was it cautionary, or might it have happened for real? How would we know?

Archaeologists in York, England who specialise in cesspit finds tell us. Articles they have written and studies they have conducted tell us that along with food scraps, seeds, and the other items one would most likely find, human remains are represented. In one of their books on this topic, Allan R. Hall and Harry K. Kenward write in the chapter "Sewers, Cesspits and Middens: A Survey of the Evidence for 2000 Years of Waste Disposal In York, UK":

> *Working within an integrated team, it was possible to study macroscopic plant remains (fruits and seeds, fragments of leaf and moss and so on), insects and other macroscopic invertebrates, the microscopic eggs of intestinal parasites, and the remains of vertebrates of all kind, including humans.*

This information was gathered and studied from archaeological deposits and included dozens of sites and hundreds of individual samples. Whether the humans were all dead when they were deposited, we don't know. One Medieval record states that a body was found in a cesspit several days after it was burned and deposited, but we know that it was a fully grown female, and it was removed. The two women responsible were caught and punished, but it was an entirely unrelated situation and had nothing to do with babies or sex.

Unwilling Partners

You're also having sex even if you're an unwilling participant. Whether during a home invasion or whilst travelling out on the roads, rape was also an unfortunate reality for the Medieval woman. Dangerous roads and drunken men have continued to be a perilous combination which can end badly for a woman who is alone, no matter the time period.

A rape leading to the actual death of a woman did not automatically lead to a conviction if the man involved was guilty, but they usually had enough jurors on their side who were prepared to say he wasn't the kind of guy to do that sort of thing. I repeat: a man might rape and kill a woman, be charged, go to court, and *still* not face the consequences of his actions.

Ellen Katemayden of Norton

Ellen's story is recorded in the *Yorkshire Sessions of the Peace* in 1363 and shows exactly a man who went to court and failed to get what he deserved.

> *The jurors present that Elias Warner of Malton on Monday after the feast of the Invention Of The Holy Cross... feloniously raped Ellen Katemayden at Malton at Norton by Malton and lay with her against her will and assaulted her and so battered her that she died within the next three days. Elias brought by the sheriff, came before the justices. The jurors came likewise, who, chosen, tried, and sworn for this, day on their oath that the aforesaid Elias is in no way*

guilty of the aforesaid felony... Therefore it is judged that the aforesaid Elias is quit thereof etc.

Talk about a cover-up. On one hand, the court stated that Elias was not only accused of rape, but felonious rape which was so brutal that the woman he attacked actually died, and then went on to say that he is quit of the charges because the other guys said he probably didn't do it. Ellen, being deceased, couldn't really stand up for herself or testify. Elias walked away unpunished.

It should be remembered that for every case which yielded someone pressing charges and going to court, a great many did not, and with results like this, you can understand why. Many women realised that there was no justice likely to be forthcoming for her and saved themselves the time and energy.

Whether repercussions were likely for the lady who attempted to stand up for herself, it isn't known. Having your rapist walk free and back into the community you both live in may not have boded well after you bring him to court in front of other men. The feeling that a woman then needed to be taught a lesson or put in her proper place made accusations dangerous, even if they were true.

Agnes de Wilton of Pocklington, Joan Smythe of Pocklington, and Ellen de Welburn of Pocklington

In the same 1363 *Yorkshire Sessions of the Peace*, one John de Warter was charged with three separate counts of breaking and entering and forced sex. The three women had their cases heard together on the same day and in front of the same jury. Might they find justice together?

The first instance was against one Agnes de Wilton, who was a single woman.

The jurors presented that John de Water of Pocklington, tailor, on Monday after the feast of the Pentecost...broke by night the home of Agnes de Wilton at Pocklington

> *and assaulted the aforesaid Agnes there and feloniously raped her.*

The second instance was against Joan Smythe, who was a married woman and wife to John Smythe.

> *Also the same jurors presented that the same John de Warter on Monday after the feast of St John the Baptist... by force of arms broke by night the door and windows of John Smythe od Pocklington and assaulted, wounded and feloniously raped Joan, the wife of the said John Smyth and against the peace etc.*

The third instance was against Ellen de Welburn, also of Pocklington.

> *Also the same jurors aforesaid presented that the aforesaid John de Warter on Monday before Christmas... feloniously raped Ellen, the daughter of John de Welburn of Pocklington etc.*

Despite three separate instances on three separate Mondays, the accused John de Warter was let off by the jury who decided:

> *The jurors came likewise, who, chosen, sworn and tried for this, say on their oath that the aforesaid John is in no way guilty of the aforesaid felonies... Therefore it is judged that the aforesaid John may go quit thereof.*

These three women had come forward and pressed charges against John, but were there others who had not? Most likely. John was now free to continue to do what he did without fear of further penalty, confident that he was most likely to be let off again whilst the women lived in fear of facing him once again. Agnes, Joan, and Ellen couldn't even feel safe in their own homes, as John had broken in each time.

All of these attacks took place on the same night of the week, Monday. Sadly, for the women of 1363 Yorkshire, Monday was not a particularly great day to be either out of home or at home.

The "Willing" Unwilling

Adding insult to injury, men accused of unsolicited sexual activity often were successful in their rebuttals against their victims by merely expressing that the woman was actually a prostitute or lying about being unwilling. He therefore lessened the punishment to the point of being non-existent and ruined her reputation whilst he was at it. As far as the law was concerned, a woman might *say* she didn't want to be raped, but he knew that actually, she really wanted it.

Rape was only particularly serious if the woman was a virgin, but again, this needed to be proven. At this point, a woman's spotless and unquestionable reputation was vital. Any question of immodest behaviour and gossip even hinting that she was a bit free with her affections was all the accused needed to back up his side of the story. She was clearly a whore. Everyone said so.

The higher up in society the lady was, the more serious the rape of a virgin. An advantageous marriage might be simply ruined if a lady was deflowered beforehand.

Agnes Webbester of Pocklington

There are innumerable records from English court rolls of cases like this, and there is no real reason that rape was confined specifically to just the English. In other cases, the felonious activity appears perplexingly side by side with other issues:

> *And they present that Thomas de Wartre, chaplain, on Monday after the feast of the Pentecost...at Pocklington feloniously ravished Agnes, the wife of William Webbester of Pocklington against the will of her husband and against the peace of the lord king and consumed and wasted the*

goods and chattels of the same William to the value of forty pence.

There are so many things going in that case, the court doesn't seem to know where to focus. Agnes was ravished, yes, but there seemed to be other great concerns:

- William was against his wife being feloniously ravished;
- the peace of the lord king was against it;
- goods were consumed; and
- chattels to the value of forty pence were also wasted.

No finding or charge was given to the outcome of that particular case, but CHATTELS WERE WASTED! In cases of abduction, the term chattels usually referred to the clothing and jewellery being worn at the time, so it is possible that the chattels which were wasted may have been torn clothing or broken dress accessories like belt buckles or brooches. Apparently, that was of as much concern as what had happened to Agnes.

It's nice that her husband was against the whole thing, but it doesn't record whether he actively fought Agnes's attackers or whether he was just not that keen on them. One supposes that the number of husbands who are *not* against their wives being attacked must be small. If the attacker was of a larger physical stature than the husband, the husband may be against it, but simultaneously be lying unconscious on the floor after being assaulted himself.

Once again, this took place after a feast day in Pocklington on a Monday. Curious.

Joan of Wiltshire

In other court cases from 1313 to 1314 in England, 142 cases were brought against men for rape. Twenty-three went to trial and only one single case was awarded to the woman who made the charges. In the case of one Joan, who did take her case to court in 1313, it ended badly for her, as it usually did for the woman. The woman complainant is named and shamed, but to protect the defendant in question, his name is represented only by his first initial, which seems a little unfair. *The Yearbook of Edward II Volume 5*, recorded the case in all its complexity.

> *Joan sued an appeal of rape against one E. who was present and the aforesaid Joan counted against him that he had lain with her in the 13th year etc and she spoke of no rape... The justice directs the court that Joan go to prison for her bad count and E. is quite of the appeal in regards to her suit, but he answers to the suit of the King. Sheriff, put him in irons.*
>
> *Justice: And you answer to the king that you raped the maid Joan who is thirty years and carries a child in her arms. The woman was asked whose the child was and she said that it was E.'s and it was said that this was a wonder because a child could not be engendered without the will of both, and it was returned that (E.) not guilty.*

Breaking it down, it appears that Joan had never known a man in the biblical sense until E. had had his way with her—either with or without her permission (but most likely without). From this event, she had fallen pregnant, and it all fell apart from there.

Current medical thought about pregnancy was that the man and the woman both needed to climax to release seed in order for a child to form, and this only happened with the wish of both parties. Pregnancy negated unwilling sex. I'd like to see that hold up in a court of law today where the pregnancy is proof positive that the encounter took place.

Undeterred, some women did at least attempt to hold their attackers accountable in a court of law; they were usually met with disappointing results even if it was common knowledge that their complaints were real and the events had actually happened.

Rose Savage of Oxfordshire

Here we meet Rose Savage, an English woman from Oxfordshire who accused a certain John de Clifford of raping her. Apparently, everyone in the town knew that the allegation was true, but unfortunately, Rose was fined by the courts for submitting incomplete and incorrect paperwork. In 1282, the level of literacy a woman might have varied substantially on who she was, but on the whole, she may have relied on someone to help her complete paperwork, and if that someone was a man, the state of her paperwork may have been deliberately sabotaged because, really, a great many men didn't like it when women stood up to them.

Oxfordshire courts in 1282 were a bit sexist, really. Incomplete paperwork? That's the best excuse you had? Really?

Callekin van Laerne of Ghent

Other courts granted that an unsavoury man may have taken carnal advantage of a woman, but they made some slightly bewildering decisions in their sentencing. The ruling of one case in fourteenth-century Ghent shows this tendency quite well.

It appeared that the feisty Callekin van Laerne had wounded a male assailant with a knife when he attempted to get up close and personal with her without her permission. The courts thoughtfully agreed that she had the right to protect herself, but hastily added that townswomen were in no way allowed to dishonour men by grabbing their buttocks.

Concealed weapons were okay, but ladies, please remember to keep your touchy-touchy hands to yourself. Duly noted.

Eleanor de Merton of London

In other more perplexing cases, men sometimes won their suits for reasons which had absolutely nothing to do with the actual case, which is a bit of an eye-opener. A letter patent from the *Patent Rolls of London* in 1348-1350 gives up this perplexing win:

> *Pardon, in consideration of good service in a late conflict at Calais, to Nicholas de Bolton of the king's suit for the rape of Eleanor de Merton, wherewith he is indicted or charged, as well as any consequent outlawry.*

What happens in Calais, apparently doesn't stay in Calais, but rewards you in other places. Apparently. This is particularly awful for poor Eleanor, as there is no dispute that he committed the rape against her, just a pat on the back for Nicholas helping out elsewhere and a Get Out Of Jail Free card.

Chapter 2

Where to Find Out About It

Getting Advice

So, where might a Medieval woman acquire good, solid advice about sex?

Today we have women's magazines like *Cleo* and *Cosmopolitan*—complete with naughty sealed sections for intimate advice. You know it's naughty because it's sealed to hint tantalisingly at the naughtiness within. It even feels naughty when you rip the pages open. Ripping pages is naughty. We've already been told. There's a sense of anticipation that we shall learn something secret and sexy.

We can also Google search anything we care to question. As most of us know, the internet has helpful advice about sexy things even when we aren't looking for it. Many parents of small children planning a themed party have been traumatised through searching for Unicorn Man and discover that although the results are quite glittery, they are not suited to the under-seven-year-old rainbow-pony-loving set. Spam folders regularly fill with unsolicited advice about performance enhancing options and members of the opposite sex who are "Eager to Meet with You and Form a Lasting Connection." The internet is extremely helpful like that.

In the modern world, just about every kind of advice can be found for lifting a libido, conception and contraceptive help for both men and women, or just finding a willing partner to engage with. Mr Right is waiting for you. Until you find him, how about Mr Right Now?

The Medieval woman had none of this, so where did she turn?

We don't know if mothers were helpful or silent on the subject, or whether the friend network sighed and giggled over whether the size of a man's lance made for a better spearing of the ring. Their words, not mine. What we do know, however, is how one particular social set felt about the whole thing, and they weren't happy at all.

The clergy.

Initial "F" with Presentation.

Beaupré Antiphonary, Vol. 3, Walters Ex Libris. W.761.folio 207v.

The Church Weighs In

Luckily for us, on the subject of sex, the church had much to say to women. We know this because they took the time and effort to carefully write it down for us for years on end. Advice about sex coming from a source of supposedly chaste men sounds like it may be less than fantastic, but quite frankly, some of it is the most fantastic and thought-provoking ever written. Relationships. Lust. Sex. Marriage. They spent a lot of time thinking about it and sharing what they thought.

Let's dip our toe in, shall we?

First, Find a Woman

The dual nature of sex caused a huge amount of mixed emotions for the men of the cloth. As far as they were concerned, there were only two types of women, really, and they loathed and loved both of them simultaneously. Women were both truly awful and yet supremely sublime. Having relations with them was to be strenuously avoided and, yet, a part of God's plan.

Tricky.

Fortunately, there were two prominent role models for each kind of woman, and they neatly embodied both ends of the spectrum of oh-how-we-love-her and oh-how-we-loathe-her. Even if you're not religious, you'll probably know who I'm talking about. Eve and Mary. Women just didn't get any better or much worse than them.

Eve of the Garden of Eden

Eve was the ultimate temptress responsible for the fall from grace of all of mankind, and quite frankly, the church was pretty annoyed with her. Clergy devoted hours and hours to writing and illuminating her in order to show exactly how awful she was. Not a single one felt she was actually just a bit naïve when she took the fruit from the tree and shared it or thought she ought to be forgiven rather than punished in the extreme.

Depending on which bible you read, Eve was the second wife of Adam, made from his own rib when his first intended wife, Lilith, who was made from earth like himself, turned out to be a bit headstrong and left the garden, refusing to return. Even the archangels sent to bring her back had no success, but they did get to have sex with her, resulting in a bunch of daughters. Or so the story goes.

Adam was extremely put out by this behaviour and demanded God make him another mate, one who would do as she was told, so God took a rib from Adam and made one. Eve was almost as disappointing as Lilith. She stayed with Adam to become his mate as he'd hoped, but she was allegedly over-fond of fruit from the Tree of Knowledge and ate more than her share—her allocated share being none at all. Eve was thenceforth punished with a swift exit from the garden for the pair of them and promised a world of hurt, bearing children for the rest of forever.

As well as the pain of childbirth, Eve can be thanked for the sin of lust, also, so at least she has that in her favour. Up until then, lust was not a thing, and the penis of Adam worked without sin like any other body part. We don't need to tell our arms or legs how to function, they just respond automatically, and it was likewise for his male member. Eve was now to blame for his lusty thoughts and the fact that Adam's penis now had a mind of its own, which is a bit of a stretch as far as handing out blame goes.

Medieval illuminators often illustrate these fabulous scenes of Adam and Eve in the garden of Eden with a snake in the tree between them. You've probably seen lots of examples, and the key elements are the same.

- Adam and Eve? Check.
- Tree between them in the middle? Check.
- Snake? Check.
- The couple are both naked? Check.

But wait a minute, take another look at the snake. There's something wrong here. You'd expect the snake to look like a regular snake, but very often in religious art of the early medieval period, the snake in the garden of Eden is shown with a head. A human head. A human lady head. How rude.

The lady-headed snake, decently attired whilst Eve has her hair out.

Temptation of Adam and Eve. ***Early fourteenth century Book of Hours, France.***

Walter's Ex Libris. W.90. folio 20r.

Amusingly, the lady-headed snake often wears a hairnet and a barbette with fillet, the standard headwear of decent women in the thirteenth and fourteenth centuries. Eve has her hair out like a total hussy. In this way, early artists are saying that even the snake in the garden of Eden is a better woman than Eve herself. That's harsh. The church viewed most women as being in the Eve category. Sinful, but necessary, but only because there were no other options for procreation, sadly.

Clement of Alexandria made no bones about it when he wrote about women generally in *Pedagogue II*.

> *Every woman should be overwhelmed with shame at the thought that she is a woman.*

He shared this view with everyone who would stand still long enough to hear it, men and women alike, so it was no real surprise that women generally had a bit of a low opinion of themselves in the early Middle Ages. Things changed a bit as the troubadours and appreciation of courtly love emerged, but at the start, if you were a woman, you were pretty much a vile necessity.

Christina da Pizzano of France

With an attitude from the church like this and a whole swathe of literature to support it, it was easy for women to come to despise themselves and put very little value on their own worth. One such woman was Christina, born in the September of 1364 in

Venice and who, when grown, became a widow whilst her child was still young. She is best known under her French name of Christine de Pisan.

The Christina who went on to become the poster girl for everything a woman should be had a very low opinion of herself initially. She agreed that women were lowly, hideous creatures, even though she herself was one. She knew this for sure because so many learned men who held low opinions of women couldn't all be wrong, right? In despair, she wrote:

> *And finally, I decided that God formed a vile creature and I wondered how such a worthy artisan could have deigned to make such an abominable work which, from what they say, is the vessel as well as the refuge and abode of every evil and vice. As I was thinking this, a great unhappiness and sadness welled up in my heart, for I detested myself and the entire feminine sex, as though we were monstrosities in nature.*

Shortly after writing this, she had a sudden vision where three ladies fetchingly attired with regal-looking crowns appeared before her and gave her a bit of a pep talk about all the wonderful and virtuous things a lady might be. They were Virtues, personified, and a vision; Reason, Rectitude, and Justice. Christine had what was essentially a light-bulb moment, then promptly embarked on a career as a writer to support herself and her child financially.

Her book, which discusses the virtues of womanhood and how to strive to be a better woman, *The Book of the City of Ladies,* became an absolute hit with women everywhere. No longer must women be seen as loathsome, but instead as gentle, caring, loving beings who possessed virtues like mercy, kindness, and charity. They might be admired, and not despised.

The Virgin Mary.
Book of Hours, Cambria 1450–1460.
Walters Ex Libris. W.240. Folio 122v

The Virgin Mary of Nazareth

On the flip side, the Virgin Mary was considered the holiest of holy women, the sublime mother of our Lord, and singlehandedly, to have generated extensive amounts of love, praise, and prayer, not to mention saleable merchandise.

She was the gold-card standard of womanhood to be admired and emulated.

Mary had a chaste marriage with her husband, Joseph, and had managed to become a mother without tainting herself by actually having to do it with a man, retaining her virginity whilst giving birth. No, really. This gained her an unattainable position, which could not actually be replicated by other living women, and the highest amount of love the church could give.

Absolutely Immaculate. Five stars. Would recommend.

This put the church in the extremely awkward position of both reviling and adoring women. Although it had strongly divergent opinions of the goodness women in general, it also recognised the need for men to marry and produce heirs. Even though the directive was to go forth and multiply, the church felt quite strongly that sex was something that a woman shouldn't have for fun. She shouldn't enjoy it. Not even maybe. Mostly, it was agreed that women were sinful and men were to avoid them where possible, especially in the bedroom. In the eleventh century, cardinal Peter Damien wrote in his *Book of Gomorrah*:

Woman is Satan's bait...poison for men's souls!

I'm pretty sure he wasn't getting any.

How to Write About It

There were a great deal of works written with sexy themes for the Medieval lady reader. Romantic poems and stories like the *Romance of the Rose* and the tale of Lancelot and Guinevere hinted at erotic liaisons.

Forbidden courtly love whispered from the pages of the unmentionable things that a lover might like to do, things that were sadly unattainable. In Guillaume de Loris' *Romance of the Rose*, or *Le Roman de la Rose*, to give it its proper French title, the characters of the story were character traits personified. Lust was a person. So was Old Age, Jealousy, and, as always, Love. Their physical attributes matched their perceived virtues or faults.

The language used in these stories is packed full of fantastic Medieval euphemisms for sexual things. And not just these books. Love had its own language. Words. Phrases. Some haven't changed ever, especially the ones referring to a man's special bit between his legs. All of those usual ones still apply. Staff. Rod. You get the idea. We can add some really great ones to those, though.

Let's learn some new ones right now, shall we? Try to slip them casually into conversation the next time things are getting hot and heavy, and see how you go.

- *Spearing the ring.* Not just a jousting term. I'll give you a clue. The lady has the ring and the man has the spear. It's in his breeches.
- *Toward the little rose.* Heading for the you-know-where. From *Romance of the Rose*.

- *Watering the curly hairs.* These are the lady hairs, and the man provides the water. This is a little weird, as the fondness for being clean-shaven was a popular concept, which we see in art.
- *Plucking the rose.* Being the first in line. You didn't need me to tell you that. It equates with the term deflowering. *Romance of the Rose* again.
- *Unfurling the petals.* Roses have petals is all I'm going to say. *Romance of the Rose.*
- *Bele chose*. *The Wife of Bath*'s literally precious thing. Thanks, Chaucer.
- *Queynte.* Chaucer Vagina. That's quite quaint, is it not?
- *Quonyam.* More Chaucer vagina. You'd never guess, would you?
- *Hole.* Chaucer gets less imaginative with this one.
- *Give a green gown.* We're talking grass stains on the back of her clothes here. It first shows up in 1351 in a Nottingham court case for rape. Written in Latin, the phrase is *induentes eam robam viridem*, which translates to "giving her a green gown." And you thought it meant that clothing was being given to a beloved lady by some very generous man. No. It wasn't.
- *Wool.* Female pubic hair. Boccaccio's tale of Griselda.
- *Pelt.* Female pubic hair. Boccaccio again.
- *Privy member.* Male or female genitals from many court cases.
- *Pudenda.* Female genitals down south. Trotula and many more.

Sexy Pictures

As always, words are not enough. When getting sexy, it's always good idea to pander to the more visual amongst us, and Medieval people were no different. Imagery in art varies from the standard sort of thing—a man and a woman in a bed either procreating or snuggling in an about-to-perform-coitus pose—to the slightly more bizarre, like women naked in bed with dragons, to the more subtle imagery of hidden meanings.

Let's go there first.

What, the Curtains?

How can one show that there's a sexual situation happening without actually showing sex? It's so easy. The use of imagery was widespread in Medieval manuscripts, with a few of the same themes cropping up repeatedly.

Many manuscripts that show tents or beds include a curtain or canopy rolled open centrally to face the viewer. Whilst bed curtains were definitely an actual thing, the point of showing them opening and rolled back in two equal folds is also symbolic of the lady in question's lower lips, which are soon to be parted in the same manner. It's sexy, but it's also just curtains.

If one isn't too sure whether this is sexually suggestive enough, the tent pole or a candle of large and impressive proportions often sits right in the middle of the folded back curtains. This hints not very subtly at the impending pole action, which is about to occur in the very near future. There's a really great one in the royal bedroom of *David and Bathsheba* in the *Morgan Bible MS M.638, fol. 41v.* The manuscript is otherwise known as the *Maciejowski Bible*, and was written in Paris around 1240. It's an enormous candle.

Once you see it in one manuscript, you can't help but noticing it forever. You're welcome.

Sex with Mythical Beasts

A more perplexing sight in Medieval manuscripts are those in-bed scenes where the crowned lady is fondly embracing a dragon whilst her anxious husband is either outside the door or looking in through a window. There's quite a few of them. They're delightful. And no, they aren't a veiled reference to bestiality or to an allegorical or a mythical tale.

Lovers of Greek mythology are used to seeing images of women copulating with animals who represent Zeus in disguise as he woos and seduces a maiden. He uses his disguise to hide from his wife and might be a bull or any number of other animals. Medieval pictures are not like this, and don't show a man transformed into something else. The animals we see are either the Devil, usually shown as a lanky black figure with pointy teeth and horns, or a dragon. A real, actual dragon. And it's supposed to be a true story. Really.

The Birth of Alexander the Great.

Walters Ex Libris. Manuscript W.307, folio 132v.

Dragon-sex pictures are meant to show the impregnation of Alexander the Great's mother Olympias by a dragon whilst his actual father Philip II looks in a window. Apparently, Alexander thought Zeus was his father because his mother had allegedly told him so. The paintings are indicating that the child born from the union was to have the heart and blood of a dragon, which would be more than a mere mortal. At no point did Alexander, who was clearly Mummy's

Special Little Man, grow into an adult with an enquiring mind who questioned the story. My dad's a dragon? Seems legit. You can find that one under *The Conception of Alexander the Great,* or *Les faize d'Alexandre (translation of Historiae Alexandri Magni of Quintus Curtius Rufus Bruges)* if you're keen. It's a nice-looking dragon, so I'd make the effort.

Pretend Sex

Of course, a woman might also pretend she's not having sex at all if having sex means having it with a man. Perhaps she needed to claim that it was all a fanciful dream, or that she was under some kind of spell or that she was attacked by demons. Sure. That's sounds convincing, right?

Jeanne Pothiere of Cambria

In 1491, Jeanne took a more slightly novel approach to having sex whilst saying she wasn't really having it by claiming that a demon appeared to her and forced her, completely against her will, to fornicate with it. Jeanne was a nun at Cambria, and the demon was in the shape of an incubi who just so happened to be an extremely handsome young man, which sounds a bit suspicious. He forced her, she claimed in all seriousness, to copulate with her four hundred and forty-four times and then forced her to introduce him to her sisters in the convent, chased them around the gardens a bit, and reduced them to climbing trees to escape his temptation.

I truly admire that Jeanne took the time out between her lovemaking to keep a tally of how many times the sexy young man forced himself upon her. It seems that at no point did she think to mention this to anyone whilst it was going on. He might have been an exceptionally cute incubi, though.

Naughty Women

Women, of course, being the lustful wanton things that they were, found themselves being painted, both literally and figuratively, in a number of unflattering ways.

Man offering a penis to a nun.

Le Roman de la Rose, ***par Guillaume de Lorris et Jean de Meun. 1301–1400, BnF Français 25526 Folio CLXr.***

The version of the *Le Roman de la Rose* from the fourteenth century in France shows several nuns picking baskets of penises growing on penis-trees in the margins of the borders in an effort to show how lustful nuns might be. Male clergy look on disapprovingly in one image, offer a penis in another, and in other images, nuns help each other out.

Another manuscript image which paints women perhaps a little unflatteringly is the 1340 to 1345 *Decretum Gratiani*, with the excellent commentary of Bartolomeo da Brescia from Italy. You can find it online under *Lyon BM Ms 5128 folio 100r*; go check it out. We find a naked woman riding an enormous penis with wings hinting not very subtly about lusty women who like to ride. You don't need to be Sigmund Freud to see that.

If this wasn't thrilling enough, some forms of jewellery took a turn for the sexy worse. Originally, pilgrim badges, which were cheap and cast in pewter of varying grades, were sold at holy places. They had holy themes, like the death of Thomas à'Beckett or the Lamb of God, or figures of saints or their relics, like Saint Catherine and her wheel.

Popular culture took this chaste reminder of a holy occasion and turned it into a series of bawdy secular badges which were the absolute height of wit and all the rage in the fourteenth century. These came in eyewatering designs; vulvas and penises being worshipped by other penises, the flying penis, penises with bells, and crowned vaginas being carried by penises with feet.

Reproduction of a secular pilgrim badge of a crowned vulva riding a horse with a flagellant whip and crossbow.

These did a roaring trade, and reproductions of them are still being made by artisans today if you know where to look. They titillated the Medieval woman and turned her thoughts towards sex.

Church-Approved Management

Having realised that men were men, and a stern talking to was in no way going to deter them from getting up close and personal with women, no matter how hard they tried, the men of the church decided that, since sex was going to happen anyway, it should happen on *their* terms. Helpful suggestions in sermons weren't cutting it. The church needed to step it up a notch.

And they did.

Chapter 3

Sex: You're Doing It Wrong

Reluctantly, the church acknowledged that a woman was required, as part of God's plan, to go forth and multiply. A birth in the parish also meant special services like baptisms, churchings (the welcoming back of a woman into society and church following the birth of a child), and monetary gifts to the church, and that was never a bad thing. A woman shouldn't, however, enjoy sexual relations. It was something to be endured for the sake of procreation.

Since sex couldn't be forbidden entirely, restrictions on when and where it could happen were set in place. Until then, couples had been getting frisky wherever and whenever the mood took them, and it seemed that this was not okay. Procreation was a business, and like all good businesses, it ought to be regulated.

Therefore, it was not permissible to have sex, even with one's own legal husband, at any of a whole heap of quite specific times. Let's count them down.

When Not to Have Sex

Sex was not permitted on a Wednesday or a Friday, for no real apparent reason that comes to mind. Both days seem incredibly arbitrary and don't seem to clash with regular religious teachings. They are fasting days, but, again, they aren't as special as Sunday. Perhaps it interfered with the Friday Night Potluck at the church hall, but we may never know.

There was no romping in the bedroom on Saturday either, which is disappointing since most people had the next day off and could stay up as late as they liked. Sunday abstinence was a given. There was absolutely no sex on a Sunday, no matter what reason you

might have. Burchard of Worms, within the Holy Roman Empire, cited a penalty of four days on bread and water if you did. People should be exclusively with the Lord and not with their spouses on Sundays.

That's already four days a week, fifty-two weeks in a year. Two hundred and eight days right there where husbands and wives were expected to Just Say No, and we've barely scratched the surface.

According to the church, Saint's feast days were quite special and needed to be observed with the proper respect, which involved being fully clothed and pure, and there were a whopping sixty of those each year. There were also public holidays, so time and opportunity gave potential for some quality lustful sinning, which needed to be stopped rather smartly.

The entire forty days of Lent should be spent in reverential contemplation and not energetic after-dark activity. Ditto the twenty days of Advent. Obviously, the twenty days of Pentecost should be similarly regarded, and definitely coitus was out of the question during Whitsun week. And don't forget the entirety of Easter week, which could extend up to ten days, depending on the year.

Whilst some of those days occurred on designated no-sex-days anyway—Wednesdays, Fridays, Saturdays, and Sundays—the amount of days marked on the calendar as unavailable for intimate rendezvous was quite substantial.

I know what you're thinking. *That's quite a list*. Coming in at around two hundred and forty days of the year without added extras. I kid you not. And there's even more to come.

Special Occasions on Which to be Chaste

To those days already listed, add another eight days. A woman could absolutely not have sex with her own husband leading up to eight days before her husband taking the eucharist. One hopes he didn't do that too often, because the number of permissible days were running low for the lady who wanted to either fall pregnant or Just Say Yes for fun. Not that she should be having it for fun anyway.Sex was also a no whilst a woman was menstruating, which was on average another forty to sixty days each year, depending on the age and diet of the woman.

Also, no sexy times whilst a woman was pregnant, which adds up another nine months right there.

Naturally, no sex whilst a woman was breastfeeding either. One wouldn't want to compromise the milk supply or start another pregnancy whilst a babe was still depending on its mother for sustenance. If you were poor, breastfeeding might be an extended situation. At least eighteen months was seen as a good thing, but in cases of poorer families, this might be extended up to two whole years. Noble ladies often employed the services of a wet nurse, which opened up the door to getting naked romantically for them personally, but closed it for the woman who was nursing the child.

Not whilst breastfeeding.

The Virgin and Child, ***Book of Hours, Walters Ex Libris. Manuscript W.428, folio 211v.***

I hope you're making note of these on your calendar.

Where Not to have It

Of course, why stop at limiting *when* a couple could be alone and naked between their linen sheets? Other instructions about locations which were out of bounds were given with as much fervour. Where should a person not have sex? Where were the no-go zones?

Common sense dictates that anywhere in public is forbidden, but these things couldn't be left to chance and needed to be spelt out specifically, just in case couples weren't too sure. Apparently, this advice not only needed to be heard, but needed to be written down, just in case it needed to be referred to at any point.

Churches prohibited sex within the walls of a church, during daylight hours, and if the woman was completely naked, and the only permissible position was what we call the missionary position. I know what you're thinking. *That's quite an interesting list. Surely that must be all. Surely, all those instructions can't be necessary?*

Let's take a look at the last couple.

No sex within the walls of a church? They had to tell people that? Were the sermons so intensely thrilling that the congregation were whipped into a frenzy of sexual excitement and couldn't wait to get home to express their passions in private? If people are in church and it's not a Sunday, then it's more than likely a Saint's Day, so it's a prohibited day for sexy times with your significant other anyway. The penalties for breaking either of those rules was a solid forty days on bread and water. Not within the church walls, then. Got it.

So...the steps out in the front were okay? How about the covered walkways on the way to the scriptorium? The herbarium at the side of the Abbott's cottage? This one raises more questions than it answers.

Amy Martynmasse of Sharnford

One court case in September 1516 from the *Episcopal Court Book for the Diocese of Lincoln* shows the misdeeds of a certain Amy who had been sinning in more than one way. She had sinned with the wrong person at the wrong time and in the wrong place and now had to pay the price for her indiscretions. The records from the church court in York show:

> *The lord bishop sitting in judgement in the chapel of his manor of Liddington ordered Amy Martynmasse of Sharnford in the county of Leicester, who was appearing before him in person and had confessed that she had been known carnally by Thomas Westmorland the curate of Uppingham within the rectory of Uppingham.*

Her punishment was thoughtfully given out:

> *...on the following Wednesday to go round the market of Uppingham publicly wearing only her chemise, her head, feet and ankles bare, holding a burning candle in her hand and to do like penance on the next two Sundays in front of the procession in the church of Uppingham and also on the third Sunday to perform like penance in Liddingham.*

One hopes it wasn't winter as hypothermia might be a very real consequence of bare feet and ankles and nothing else but a white chemise made of linen. Even very thick linen would offer almost no protection against the elements. Public shaming was somehow appropriate for Amy, but no penance was given to the curate, Thomas, who presumably got little more than a rap over the knuckles or some secret high fives. The sentence also implies that Amy wasn't a victim of her spiritual father, when most other indications and court cases suggest that the men involved took advantage of housekeepers and parishioners alike.

The no sex in the church rule was, of course, clearly meant only for the general public.

The Woman from the Alps

Salimbene di Adamo, a Franciscan monk who was born in Parma in 1221, at one stage worked for a local noble family and was charged with writing cautionary stories for the family's fifteen-year-old niece so that she might avoid falling prey to wayward clergyman and their lusty ways. Sadly, we don't know the name of the young lady, who wasn't deemed important enough to write down. Salembine had cautionary and apparently true stories to use as examples of exactly how lecherous people were in general, but he also felt it wasn't necessary to give names to these women. Perhaps he was protecting their privacy. He knew of a woman, he said, who came to confession, but he does not say her name, only that she was from the alps. He tells her story.

> *A certain woman confessed to her priest that she had been violated by a stranger in a lonely place in the alps where she lived. The priest made probing enquiries into the exact nature of the violations and became so excited that he dragged the woman off and raped her himself. Apparently, her tears and distress at the original encounter were not any kind of deterrent. She went on to confess to a second and third priest who again behaved exactly the same as the first one. Undeterred, the woman sought out a fourth and confessed to him. He gave her absolution but not before noticing that she had a knife which she intended to kill herself with if he also cruelly misused her.*

One can barely begin to understand the kind of apprehension this woman must have had in wanting to confess her crime and be forgiven after the treatment at the hands of her first confessor. Then the second. How she braved a third is a testament to her faith that surely there were good men of God to reach out to. Her utter despair at preparing to take her own life after the

third confession attempt went badly tells us so much. Suicide is never the easy way out.

The Woman Who Made the Pie

Salimbene told a further story, also supposedly true, to illustrate further how even men of the cloth could not be trusted. In this one, the woman, also unnamed, comes out the best. The woman confesses her sins and the priest puts the hard word on her then and there. She refuses and says to him that there are more convenient times and places than this. The priest is greatly encouraged by this and promptly sets up a rendezvous at the woman's house in the very near future.

Man at a feast. *Psalter and Office of the Dead. Walters Ex Libris. Manuscript W.117, folio 3r.*

Meanwhile, she sends him a gift of a bottle of wine and a homemade pie in advance. The priest, hoping to get in the good books of the bishop, passes them on to him, which is extremely unfortunate as it turns out the woman has filled the empty wine bottle with her urine and filled the pastry of the pie with excrement. When asked to explain, the red-faced priest tried to pass off the lady's gifts as a hilarious, light-hearted trick, but when the woman is asked to explain to the bishop herself, she makes no bones about explaining what was really going on. She went unpunished. The friar, however, had to answer to Pope Alexander IV who was not impressed.

The Dark Ages

Restricting sex during daylight hours makes a certain amount of practical sense. During daylight hours, a woman should be gainfully employed in domestic activity either inside her home, cooking and cleaning or sewing and spinning, or outside her home with any number of domestic chores involving vegetables or miscellaneous types of poultry.

Since windows were small and interior lighting was often poor and expensive, the most ought to be made of the productive daytime hours. Frittering them away on encounters likely to make babies was a waste of valuable time better spent on household management.

No sex whilst you're pregnant might seem the easiest rule to understand, although extremely unfair. A woman's delicate condition was rarely an excuse to not do something. In the family home of working-class women, chores must still continue, herb gardens must be tended, chickens fed, cows milked; daily life was, well, no different. It seems a little unfair to single the sexy-times activity out.

The benefit of pregnancy sex was that a woman couldn't fall pregnant a second time if she was pregnant already, which is probably why it was frowned upon. Nevertheless, the penalty for sex after the foetus had stirred and the pregnancy was confirmed was twenty days on bread and water. Whilst it seems a light punishment compared to many others, it's hardly a nourishing diet for an unborn child. If morning sickness is an issue for the mother-to-be, bread and water might be the only things staying down, so it could be worse.

The Wrong Time of the Month

As far as the church was concerned, the wrong time of the month was definitely the wrong time of the month for getting naked with one's husband and doing it. Having sex whilst you're menstruating is one sin which attracted a comparatively slight ten-day punishment of bread and water penance. Very early copies from Lindisfarne insisted that forty days was more appropriate, but by the later medieval period, it was more usual to be given ten.

Portrait of the Venerable Bede.

Homilary, Walters Ex Libris. Manuscript W.148, folio 3v.

Many modern women don't hold with getting sexy at that time of the month. It's sometimes seen as a bit gross or messy. Many twenty-first century women choose to adopt the hot-water-bottle-and-chocolate approach to evenings at home rather than the slip-into-lingerie-and-give-the-come-hither to their partners approach to their periods. Others don't care. It's a personal choice, so whatever works for you is fine.

Being told you are forbidden by some overbearing, supposedly celibate man in a frock is not.

The Venerable Bede's penitential, which was written somewhere around the year 700 AD, not only discouraged getting intimate with menstruating women who had their so-called sickness, but actively punished it more than others. He handed out a fairly stern forty days' penance. He felt that the bible was pretty clear about these things in Leviticus:

> *If a man shall lie with a woman having her sickness, and shall uncover her nakedness; he hath discovered her*

> *fountain, and she hath uncovered the fountain of her blood: and both of them shall be cut off from amongst their people.*

The most shameful thing about period sex is that the writers kept insisting that it was shameful. Untidy, maybe, but not shameful. The use of the word fountain is great, too. It might feel an accurate description for those super heavy days, but in real terms of blood loss, one could hardly call it a fountain.

We don't know if Medieval women were concerned with the untidiness of the actual act at that time, but practitioners of Medieval medicine believed that menstrual blood was highly toxic and quite likely to mutilate sperm. Contemporary science insisted intercourse at the time of the month of the menses would birth a mutilated child rife with any number of hideous diseases—leprosy, epilepsy, or worse. It might even produce...a... red headed child.

And no one wants that.

How to Have It

Only the missionary position was sanctioned as the correct way to have sex. In case you were unsure how to do it or what that was, manuscripts helpfully provided pictures.

The most well known health handbook, the *Tacuinum Sanitatus*, is the most sensible of all of the books that contained pictures. It was circulating in the fourteenth and fifteenth centuries. Several copies survive to this day. The *Tacuinum Sanitatus* use almost full-page colour illustrations to depict a number of foods and natural elements which impact a person's good health. These include foods, but also elements like the North Wind, Vomiting, Dancing, and, of course, Coitus.

Coitus is drawn in full colour with a man and a woman in bed and a particularly flimsy coverlet, which allowed the reader to see what position the legs should be in for both the man and the

woman for successful, proper baby making. It's the one we call the missionary position.

None other was recommended and all others were varying degrees of sinful for a variety of great reasons. Copulating as animals do from behind was a no. Woman-on-top? Also no. Everything else was also a no. Just the missionary position. The lads in the pulpit said so.

The reasoning behind this was based on what medicine knew to be true of the human body and its reproductive systems. Should the woman be on top, seed would not travel in the right direction, and conception might be prevented, making the whole activity a complete waste of time. Coupling with your wife *retro canino*, that is, doggy style, was also sinful because it emulated the beasts of the field, and you'd be regretting it on bread and water for the next ten days. Generally, any position which lessened the chance of procreation was sinful.

Magnus, who wrote quite a bit about medical things pertaining to procreation and a plethora of other topics also instructed:

> *They should not have intercourse lying on their sides, because then the seed is poured on one side of the womb and as a result is wasted and generation is prevented.*

and...

> *They should not do it standing up, because then the seed is projected upwards and afterwards falls down.*

...which is quite helpful if you were getting a little bored with the missionary position but didn't have any ideas yourself. Despite the missionary position being the recommended and church-approved way to couple, there are many images of what not to do in Medieval literature.

Images, particularly of hell and purgatory, show the very things people can go to hell for, including many sexual acts and positions. To go with the images, there are some really fabulous descriptions and euphemisms for the act of coupling and the body parts required. Many of these use words that today we not only consider to be uncouth, but downright offensive, including one starting with C. This word was a common noun at the time and no more uncouth than naming any other body part like arm, leg, or face.

Man and nun standing up for sex.

Marginalia from* Le Roman de la Rose, *par Guillaume de Lorris et Jean de Meun. Dated between 1301 and 1400. Held in the Département des manuscrits. Français. Gallica BnF 25526. Folio CXIr.

How to Dress for It

Dressing in an alluring manner for some sexy times in the bedroom is an important consideration for many women today, and it's no great surprise that Medieval women also dressed for sex in a properly appealing and therefore alluring way.

Of course, they did. Why wouldn't they?

When most modern people think of Medieval ladies, they immediately think of chastity belts and corsets! That sounds sexy, doesn't it? It sounds erotic and a little bit fetishist. The problem with this is that neither of these garments had been invented in the early medieval period and only made their first appearances in late Tudor and the early Renaissance. In the case of chastity belts, even later.

"But it was in a book I read," I hear you cry, "It said corset!"

You'd be right about the corsets being in books. Written inventories *do* mention them, but unfortunately, the item of clothing written in accounts isn't what we call a corset today. Let me explain. The tricky thing with history is that often the *name* of something has been around for a long time, but the *thing* the name belongs to has changed and no longer means what it originally did.

In this way, the corset is both Medieval and also not Medieval.

Concerning Corsets

Written clothing accounts from the fourteenth century from both England and Europe do mention corsets. The wardrobe accounts of Edward the Black Prince describe them and amounts of fabrics for them, the type of decoration they had, and who they were made for. It's quite a lot of information. They were such a garment which was so easily recognised, that specifics about what they looked like is *not* recorded.

We understand what a shirt or hose looks like. Corsets, then, also needed no special explaining to the Medieval person. They were a garment which was known and understood. When we look at what was used to make them and who was wearing them, however, all signs point to them not being the kind of garment we call a corset today. What *do* we know?

These were special occasion garments, worn as an outer layer. They were usually highly decorated, and we know from the amount of fabric used to make them that they were not fitted, and some had a train. Indeed, there were more than one type, and some were suited for dancing in. The fact that corsets were made for young boy princes should be a big heads-up right there that perhaps they aren't a sexy undergarment.

That corsets are highly decorated with pearls and gold thread also indicates that they are designed to be seen and to

impress everyone with their richness. Garments like this were always worn as a top layer. To spend money on conspicuous consumption where it couldn't be seen was a pointless waste of money. Nevertheless, in reading that the princes wore them on special occasions, many modern people have decided that this should be interpreted that young boys wore restricting undergarments called corsets of the type familiar to us today.

I'm pretty sure that's not what happened. Even in other languages, the *corset fendu* is the phrase describing what we call a *sideless surcote* today. It is quite possible that the corset that was worn in the fourteenth century was an overgown with large armholes either with or without a train.

The most telling of all is that, when the undergarment we know today as a corset first appears in texts, it is referred to as a *body* or a *pair of bodies* and then later as *stays*. After that, *corset* becomes the popular word meaning the laced up, tight, bosom-enhancing garment we know today.

So, corsets? No. Not the kind you're thinking of.

Gratuitous Nudity

We already know the church had clear sentiments about not having relations whilst you're naked, so what's that all about? Surely nudity and sex go hand in hand! If a Medieval woman couldn't wear a corset, why couldn't a woman be naked instead?

Why? It's very simple. It was believed, medically, that most of the heat in the female body was lost through the head, and during the vigorous ardours of coitus, a woman may lose far too much heat, far too suddenly. Calamity would befall her. Any number of ailments might suddenly occur. It needed to be addressed. Complete nudity had to be avoided at all costs.

The Medieval woman needed to dress appropriately for sex. She could be mostly naked, but not entirely. Especially her head. For the benefit of her continued good health, the exertions of

Birth of the Virgin.

Missal of Eberhard von Greiffenklau, Walters Ex Libris. Manuscript W.174, folio 204v.

romping enthusiastically between the sheets with her husband should be countered by wearing some kind of coif. Or veil. Or turban. Even a hairnet would do, which is bordering on the ridiculous. As long as some kind of a token effort was being made, it was safe to continue.

This is why, in manuscripts that show a man and woman in bed together, you will notice that any decent lady is almost certainly wearing some kind of head covering.

Ladies, you can leave your hat on!

Chapter 4

Kissing and Telling: Church Confessionals and What We Learn

Policing It

Clearly, with so many restrictions on what goes on in the bedroom—with your own husband, after dark, whilst not entirely naked, on an approved day—some kind of policing of these rules was required. Rules are utterly useless unless people are regularly checked up on.

Obviously, some selfless individual needed to step up and shoulder this burden, but whom? Who was there to tackle this thankless task and deal with flagrant disobedience or lapses with the moral compass? Who, indeed?

Here also, the church was standing by to help. Standing by. Insisting. Whatever.

The Confessional

We are fortunate that the world of the church was an extremely literate one. Many religious texts survive which have been handed down, carefully re-copied throughout the years, and dutifully passed around from monastery to monastery, library to library, and church to church. These were the penitentials; the books that priests used in the confessionals to enquire about a person's sins and hand out the appropriate punishment. One

only needed to admit to being guilty and being sorry about it. Sometimes prompting was needed.

Manuscripts and books used by priests for the questioning of the hapless parishioners have been around for an extremely long time. Some were listed amongst personal possessions of parish priests. Others which are simply written and undecorated show heavy wear and tear, which indicates that they were well-used and often referred to.

Bishop from a hymnal.

Walters Ex Libris. Manuscript W.547, folio 220v.

Amongst those texts, instructions for priests in the church confessional still come to us today. As you'd imagine, in a time of sexual restriction, questions seemed unnecessarily explicit, and the church confessional became an increasingly personal experience for both men and women.

Personal, bordering on intrusive, one might say. Hand in hand with this were discussions as to the correct manner of asking questions, so as not to plant seeds of sinful behaviour where there were formerly none. I mean, one wouldn't want to give people ideas or anything.

Burchard's Corrector

Priests could and did ask the most delicate questions about a woman's most intimate practices. In the eleventh century, a German confessor's manual, *Le Corrector sive Medicus*, known in English as *The Corrector* or *The Doctor*, was written by the extremely thorough Burchard of Worms, who diligently concerned himself with an enormous amount of sexual practices. Burchard was born sometime between 950 and 965 AD and rose to the heady rank of Deacon in the Catholic church. He

singlehandedly wrote twenty books, each with a religious theme of important matters concerning men and women and affairs of the soul.

Burchard was a middle child, and if he was trying to get himself noticed, he certainly did. A statue of him can be found outside St Peter's Cathedral in Rome today. His prolific writings include his fabulous *Confessor's Manual*, and it is that with which we shall acquaint ourselves.

This lengthy compendium of questions pertained to men and their unnatural practices, but an astounding amount of the questions were directed specifically at women. Volume nineteen, chapter five offers a staggering one hundred and ninety-four sexy questions to ask. How priests managed to get through them all without committing self-violations of their own is an absolute wonder.

From that exciting list of misdemeanours, I've chosen my top personal favourite Burchard of Worms confessional queries to share with you. These range in a varying degree of invasion of privacy, starting with practices which may have actually happened to the outright bizarre.

Feel free to answer them quietly to yourself as we go.

Taste Tests

Let's start with most understandable of his sins regarding sex practices, which was aimed specifically at women:

> *Have you tasted your husband's semen in order to make his love for you burn greater through your diabolical deeds? If you have, you should do seven years of penance on the appointed fast days.*

Seven years! Seven *years!* That's a huge amount of time for something as simple as oral sex with someone you married. Diabolical, it may be, but I imagine a number of husbands are

quite behind this one as far as abominable practices go and would rather Burchard just keep it to himself. It's an entirely valid assumption that a husband's love actually *will* burn brighter for the lady who likes to lick.

But what of the reluctant lady? How might a husband talk her into it if she's feeling doubtful?

Finally, it's the right day of the week, and it's no particular religious holiday, and the opportunity is there... John and Christina are having some quality alone time...things are getting hot and heavy...

John: *Oh, Christina, I love your kisses...*

Christina: *Oh John! Any wish you have, and desire, I shall fulfil for you as a wife should do.*

John: *Darling wife, my love, there is one thing.*

Christina: *As your obedient wife, my love, anything!*

John whispers in her ear.

Christina: *(Shocked) John! I mustn't! Why just this morning, Brother Edward said that I mustn't!*

John: *Are you sure you heard him right? He didn't say you must?*

Christina: *I'm pretty sure he said "mustn't."*

John: *Are you really, really positive?*

Christina: *No, he was quite clear. I mustn't taste your seed. It is forbidden!*

John: *But I'm your husband! Please? For me?*

Christina: *Surely not! I will burn in the pits of hell! I mustn't taste...*

Crickets chirping.

John: *So just swallow?*

Damn Burchard, ruining it for the rest of them.

Whilst that particular question had probable cause and might truthfully be answered in a manner incurring a fasting and prayer penalty, other questions were less likely to be actually true and centred heavily around women inflaming their husband's sexual desires, presumably against their will.

This seems to indicate that Burchard of Worms felt that is was only *the women* who were the lustful instigators of marital relations and that the husbands needed encouraging. A short survey of twenty-first century men showed that this was unlikely to be correct.

Alternatively, perhaps he felt that the reluctant husband, who was having sex forced on him against his own will, needed to have his desire increased towards his *own* wife and away from *other* lustful women who were certainly begging for it every time he left the house. Women being the foul temptresses they were, and all.

Buns in the Ovens

The delightful Burchard either had a great number of members of his congregation with exciting sex lives giving him ideas or quite a lively imagination. He may have been exceptionally overly hopeful when he asked:

> *Have you done what some women are accustomed to do? They take off their clothes and smear honey all over their naked body. With the honey on their body they roll themselves back and forth over wheat on a sheet spread on the ground. They carefully collect all the grains of wheat sticking to their moist body, put them in a mill, turn the mill in the opposite direction of the sun, grind the wheat into flour, and bake bread from it. Then they serve it to their husbands to eat, who then grow weak and die. If you have, you should do penance for forty days on bread and water.*

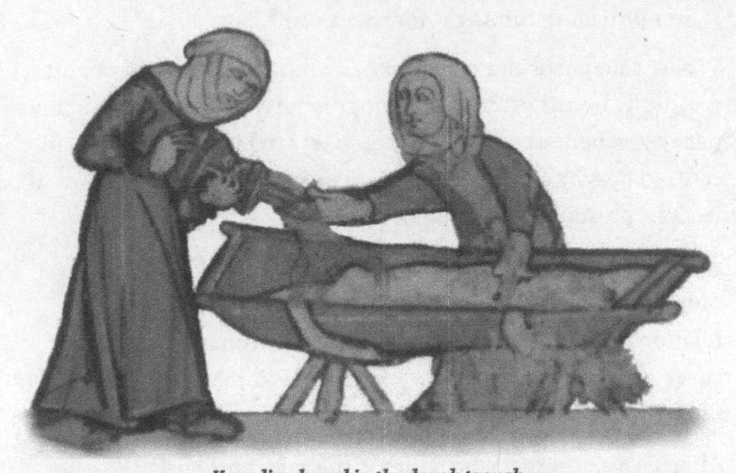

Kneading bread in the dough trough.

Book of Hours, Flanders, early fourteenth century. Walters Ex Libris. W88 folio 15r.

The smearing honey bit sounds like it might be a fine way to spend a quiet night in, but it may use up an entire week's worth of honey in one sitting. Or naked rolling, as it were.

One also assumes that if the grains of wheat are to be collected, one may require the services of a helpful friend to get into those crevices which are hard to reach. And all this to weaken him and make him die? If he found out about it, he'd be more likely to die of excitement than anything else. Unless he had some serious gluten allergies going on.

Forty days' penance for the bread-related demise of a spouse seems quite lenient and well worth the effort if a woman was trapped in a loveless marriage and could spare the honey. Just saying. On a more practical note, the compliance of a very helpful friend with whom a woman is close enough to ask for assistance with honey-smearing is necessary.

Burchard obviously has a bit of a thing for bread and is particularly down on baked goods because he doesn't stop at grains of wheat when it comes to the opportunities a woman might take when it comes to bread. He continues:

> *Have you done what some women are accustomed to do? They lie face down on the ground, uncover their buttocks, and tell someone to make bread on their naked buttocks. When they have cooked it, they give it to their husbands to eat. They do this to make them more ardent in their love for them. If you have, you should do two years of penance on the appointed fast days.*

If a lady had a very special someone whom she desired very much, this is certainly something to consider. As with the last item, it was not a thing a woman could accomplish alone. It was an activity which required at least two ladies, one of whom already needed to know what to do.

> *Alice and Margery are chatting at the village well whilst they draw water for the day. Margery is expressing concern that her husband has been distracted of late and wondering if she might spice things up in the bedroom.*
>
> **Alice:** *Spice things up? Spices are expensive. Have you considered breading up instead?*
>
> **Margery:** *Ummm. What?*
>
> **Alice:** *Bread. Have you tried using bread?*
>
> **Margery:** *Well, I do give him bread every day.*
>
> **Alice:** *Not the right kind of bread. I can show you how to make the right kind of bread.*
>
> **Margery:** *Really? You're the best friend! How do I make it?*
>
> **Alice:** *Well first, you need to lie face down with your butt naked, then...*
>
> **Margery:** *Wait, what?*
>
> **Alice:** *...then I'll knead the dough on them and we can bake it afterwards!*
>
> **Margery:** *And this will make him desire me more?*

> **Alice:** *Brother Edward asked me in the confessional, and he seems certain that this is so.*
>
> **Margery:** *Well...he should know!*
>
> **Alice:** *And if it doesn't make him desire you more, it will bring us closer together.*
>
> **Margery:** *Oh, Alice!*
>
> **Alice:** *I also have a really great recipe for a honey bun if that doesn't work.*

So, let me get this straight. Forty days' penance for attempted murder with honey loaf, but two entire years fasting and prayer for passion-inflaming buttock-bread? It seems a bit arbitrary. Wouldn't it have been better to just invite the husband to the naked portion of the activity and skip the bread-baking altogether? No?

Fishing for Compliments

It doesn't stop there when it comes to consumables and sex. Another gem from the pen and ink of Burchard of Worms is question 172, where he takes the things a woman might do with food a step further and asks in all apparent seriousness:

> *Did you do what some women are used to doing: they take a live fish, introduce it into their vagina, and hold it there until it is dead; and after cooking or grilling this fish, they feed it to their husbands so that it ignites more love for them? If so, you will do penance for two years on the appointed days.*

What? *Some women* are used to doing? *What* women? Seriously, what women are used to doing that?

Initial M with Annunciation.

Beaupré Antiphonary, Vol. 1, Walters Ex Libris. Manuscript W 759, folio 108r.

Questions like this seem unlikely to give a lovelorn lady ideas about recreating them, much less to admit to doing them. From the amount of women-have-fishy-smelling-private-parts jokes circulating, one might understand how a fish inserted might seem like a valid question. Disappointingly, it fails to mention whether a specific type of fish is required or whether anything which swims in the water counted as a fish.

Thursday afternoon, and Alice is at the fish market picking up a little something for dinner the following day.

Fishmonger: *Can I help you there?*

Alice: *I'm after a little something for dinner tomorrow.*

Fishmonger: *Do you see anything that takes your fancy?*

Alice: *Well, there's so many to choose from but I need something rather specific.*

Fishmonger: *How about herring? Nice and fresh!*

Alice: *Oh no. That's won't do. Far too small.*

Fishmonger: *How about plaice? Pike?*

Alice: *Umm, no. No...*

Fishmonger: *Dolphin?*

Alice: *Oh, no! I could never!*

Fishmonger: *Well...well, I do have eel?*

Alice: *Oooooooh! Eel, you say! Oh my! Is it fresh?*

Fishmonger: *So fresh it's still alive!*

Alice: *SOLD!*

Many texts about Medieval diets tell us that any beast which goes in a river, pond, or the sea counts as a fish in regard to Friday Fish Days, so there's food for thought. Or for inserting. Apparently.

Marginalia. Incomplete Book of Hours, Walters Manuscript W 87, folio 20v.

Food for Thought

And finally, an absolute favourite Burchard of Worms question which demonstrates exactly what kind of women he thought he was dealing with:

> *Have you done what some women are wont to do? They take their menstrual blood, mix it into food or drink, and give it to their men to eat or drink to make them love them more. If you have done this, you should do five years of penance on the appointed fast days.*

You have got to be kidding me.

Now there's a *MasterChef* episode I don't need to see right there. Five years of penance. Five. Years. It raises so many questions. What kind of food? Exactly how much menstrual blood is needed to get a really effective result? No question more important than

the hypothetical—if a woman is bleeding enough to gather her blood, isn't sex completely out of the question that night? And what about the taste? Not a single cookery book from the Middle Ages has advice on what herbs one might need to mask that!

Margaret is busy at the hearth preparing dinner. Her husband Edward sits eagerly at the table.

Edward: *Mmmm, something smells good? What's for dinner?*

Margaret: *It's pie! I made it especially for you.*

Edward: *Oh great! I love your pie!*

Margaret: *I bet you will.*

Edward takes a bite.

Margaret: *It's good isn't it? Eat up, darling!*

Edward: *You're not having any?*

Margaret: *I'm…uh…not hungry. Yes. That's it. I filled up on cheese earlier.*

Edward: *Suit yourself. Mmmm… It's pretty great.*

Takes another bite.

Edward: *Uh…it tastes a little…different…uh…Margaret, what's in it?*

Pours "red" wine.

Margaret: *Oh, nothing! Just my Special Sauce! Eat up!*

Also, why did he ask this? Exactly how many women confessed to this exceptionally dubious practice in order for a decision to be made to write it down? How did this make the list? I'm just guessing, but I'm fairly confident when I say that no woman ever responded with a "Oh, heck! Who told you?"

Seriously, how did that last question even make it to the list? Was there a meeting amongst the monks which was fuelled by a little

too much communion wine? Surely this wasn't a decision made by sober, educated humans!

A meeting of learned men, monks, brothers, and clerics are gathering for their annual weekly meeting and debrief. Beverages and snacks are being dispensed, but mostly beverages.

Brother Edward: *Welcome, everyone, to the St Mark's Parish weekly staff meeting. We have a number of issues on the table to get through, so we'll start with some refreshment.*

Pours more wine.

Right! Everyone set? Cheers! This week we're going to finalise the list of questions we're putting into the new confessional. Suggestions, anyone?

Brother Adrian: *How about the one about coveting asses?*

Brother Edward: *We've got that, already, but thank you.*

Brother Christos: *Do we have the one about worshipping images?*

Brother Edward: *We've got that, but thank you.*

Brother Burchard: *The one about putting the menstrual blood into the food?*

Brother Edward: *We've got tha...wait...WHAT did you say?*

Brother Burchard: *Well, I was in the confession last week and a woman said unto me that she had mixed her menstrual blood into some food and cooked it and served it to her husband that he might desire her more. Have we got that one? I don't think we have that one. You'd better write that down.*

Crickets chirping.

Brother Edward: *You don't suppose that's just her, Brother Burchard?*

Brother Damien: *Women ARE Satan's bait, Brother Edward. They're probably ALL doing it.*

Crickets chirping.

Brother Edward: *...hmmm...*

Writes it down.

Okay, hands up, ladies, who has been mocking the priests by making stuff up in the confessional?

St Ecgbert of Lindisfarne Weighs In

Burchard wasn't the only one to spend quality time thinking about what might be going on in the bedroom. St Ecgbert, the Bishop of Lindisfarne, also wrote extensively on the subject. He also felt that bodily fluids and food might be a problem, but he was not too sure about whether this practice was restricted to womanly fluids or fluids of everyone involved. He asked whether the woman might have mixed her husband's sperm into food. He felt quite strongly that this might increase the woman's desire towards the man whose sperm it was. Only three years of fasting and prayer for this one, a good two years less than the menstrual blood one. Manly fluids are less offensive, somehow, in the deserving of punishment stakes.

The fact that the church felt the need to ask these and a plethora of other questions tells us a certain amount about sex practices both real and imagined which were frowned upon, even if they didn't involve sex with men.

Chapter 5

Getting Physical

Health and Sex

Now, it wasn't all bad news for the ladies.

According to medical beliefs in the Middle Ages, sex was a requirement for an adult woman's ongoing good health. Not an option. A requirement. If she didn't receive the correct amount of good loving, she would definitely suffer a staggering variety of health problems. Disappointingly, this is a theory which has been discontinued in the twenty-first century, although we do realise that there are some health advantages to a natural dopamine hit which comes from sex. Happiness, for one.

To understand the Medieval belief of needing coitus for good health as a woman, a quick look at what contemporary medicine had to say about the interior sex organs is in order. Galen of Pergamon, who was the considered expert in the Roman Empire sometime before 215 BCE, and who wrote extensively of anything and everything medical, was pretty certain he knew what was going on.

> *Think first, please, of the man's (genitals) turned in and extending inward between the rectum and the bladder. If this should happen, the scrotum would necessarily take the place of the uteri, with the testes lying outside, next to it on either side.*

Essentially, he was sure that the female sexual organs perfectly mirrored the male sexual organs, only they were inwards, not outwards. The male bit which dangled out equalled the female bit which tucked inwards. The scrotum and testes were the equivalent of the ovaries. It actually sounds quite reasonable.

He was so persuasive in his writings that many of his theories, including this one, were still widely regarded as correct into the late Middle Ages. His works were continually incorporated into later works of medicine. Once these ideas got around, they were incredibly hard to get rid of.

The Wandering Womb

One of the most fabulous medical theories which kicked off with the ancient Greeks and just wouldn't die was that of the wandering womb. Galen wasn't a fan himself, but the Greek doctor Aretaeus was a firm believer. It's hard to imagine how a theory like this was suggested in the first place, let alone discussed between learned men and then shared with others who were inquisitive enough to ask. There was quite a bit of debate about it.

The crux of the matter was that no one could agree whether the womb was a stationary organ and stayed in situ the entire time like other bodily organs or whether the womb was much more active and wandered around the female body collecting toxins and causing problems until it returned to her pelvic region. Only then might a woman purge her menses.

It seemed that no other organs were wanderers, so it was given special consideration. Whilst it meandered haphazardly around the body, the womb might cause any number of other ailments. A headache might be caused by the womb stuck in the head. Shortness of breath was certainly caused by the womb stuck under the ribs. You get the idea.

Now, if a woman's womb wandered around her body during the month, and then needed to be anchored in the proper place so her period could occur, *how* should this occur? I'm glad you asked. The answer is *with sex*. Sex would bring a womb back to its correct place. A woman needed it for her good health.

Hooray!

The Four Humours

According to the very popular and forward-thinking four humours school of medical thought, which was uppermost during the Middle Ages, women were also notoriously lusty, if not downright insatiable.

It was Galen of Pergamon's *Doctrine of Humours* which advocated that four humours and four elements were linked to every aspect of human physical health, and this was still widely followed in the medieval period.

The four humours were blood, phlegm, yellow or red bile, and black bile, and the four elements were hot, cold, wet, and dry. The combinations of these things was directly responsible for good health or ailments and treatments were given accordingly. Galen believed that women were cold and men were hot and that both of these conditions required decisive action to balance them.

Cold Women

Women being *cold* caused a number of unhappy medical conditions, including weakened eyes, headaches, and dryness of the vagina. Apparently, the excuse "Not tonight dear, I have a headache!" should be remedied with having sex, something that modern medicine actually feels to be a bit valid.

Endorphins released during intercourse are quite beneficial to headaches, although it's negated by the lack of desire to actually have it in the first place. It's ironic that the term *frigid* when applied to a woman today has connotations that she is either unwilling or not desirous of sex and as cold as an iceberg, whereas in the Medieval sense, a cold woman meant that she craved it.

Oversexed Women

Lusty women also faced other, more terrible medical complains. Magnus, in his writings in *The Secrets of Women*, explained that a mole might grow in the womb of the woman who was not having the proper amount of intercourse. He wrote:

> *This happens to many young women who are incapable of performing the venereal act because of the small opening of their womb. When they are in bed asleep at night lying on their backs the exceeding attraction and desire that they experience causes them to have an emission of their own seed. This pollution remains in their body near the umbilicus and grows into a large mass of flesh, so that their abdomen begins to swell and they believe mistakenly that they are pregnant. This type of tumour, called by doctors the mole of the womb, can be cured by medical regimen.*

It is unknown whether a large number of women suffered from abdominal cancers which prompted these thoughts, but it seems that a good deal of thought was being given to it, whatever it was. It probably wasn't lack of sex, though. My thoughts, not his.

Undersexed Women

If that wasn't bad enough, a woman who failed to get enough sex risked the humours building up inside her, leading to certain madness, convulsions, fainting fits, suffocation of the womb, and hysteria. It seemed that the right amount of proper sex, on the right days and at the right times, of course, was required. A woman *needed* regular sexual intercourse for her emotional and physical well-being. If her womb wasn't adequately anchored, all manner of ills might befall her, and no one wanted that. Women were tricky enough as it was without the added benefit of an unanchored bit.

Failure to Perform

Because of this, a husband's impotency was taken quite seriously. Very seriously. So seriously, that a woman could divorce or have her marriage dissolved from a man for his inability to perform in the bedroom.

I feel that's a rule we should bring back. A quick show of hands, ladies? I thought as much.

Margaret Maultasch of Tyrol

There are quite a few fourteenth- and fifteenth-century court cases where women have divorced their husbands for their failure to satisfy in the marital bed. Margaret Maultasch was born in 1318 in Austria, and she was one of them. The rather disappointed Margaret was Countess of Tyrol when she did exactly that to her under-performing husband Henry of Bohemia in 1340.

She filed and won her annulment, which left her free to hook up with someone she really fancied. Louis of Brandenburg, we're looking at you.

Now, it's a tempting thought to just point the finger at a husband you weren't particularly fond of and get that annulment. Perhaps a woman might have a spouse who was old and unattractive, whom that upwardly-mobile woman with social aspirations had married. She might accuse him of neglecting her health by not performing in the bedroom, and get that divorce to free her up for that cute recently-widowed landowner next door.

For health reasons, of course.

Divorce being the serious matter it was in the Middle Ages in both secular and religious courts, you'd like to hope that there was some kind of a test where an accused husband could refute false claims. After all, his assets were involved, not to mention his reputation. But mainly the assets. It would be grossly unfair for it to come down to a matter of her word against his, especially

when women were generally having a bit of a tough time of it in law courts generally. On the woman's side, she'd certainly need proof, wouldn't she?

Some kind of test, perhaps?

And what luck. There absolutely *was* a test to check if an under-performing husband was unable to adequately discharge his marital duty to his wife. I kid you not in the least. There are documented court cases as early as 1292 in Canterbury and as late as 1433 in the county of York in England, where women testified against their husbands in cases such as these and won.

Bedroom Trials

I particularly like that not only did these cases go to court, but that they were carefully recorded with names and dates and who said what and when. One Thomas of Chobham, who was Sub-dean at the Salisbury Cathedral at the time, devised a method to determine if a husband was absolutely impotent and this became the usual method of trial in cases like these.

It began with a physical examination of the man's genitals, although whether by a medical professional or by the court itself, is unclear. One hopes for a medic. Wearing gloves. We aren't told exactly what the criteria should be to pass this examination either, only that it needed to be passed before the next step in the trial could begin.

The next step was the bedroom trial proper. Thomas instructed how this should be carried out.

> *After food and drink, the man and the woman are to be placed together in one bed and wise women are to be summoned around the bed for many nights. And if the man's member is always found to be useless and as if dead, the couple are well to be separated.*

Gratian's Decretum, ***Historiated initial "Q" showing a canonist hearing the case of an impotent man whose wife left him and remarried another man, but then returned to her first husband when his impotence was cured, Walters Manuscript W.133, folio 277r.***

One supposes that unless having an audience was especially a man's thing, performance anxiety may have been a very real issue, and perhaps if, until then, his performance had not been lacking, even the bravest man might falter at this point. Thus, bedroom trials were doomed for failure before they even began.

Let's stand by and see how it all happened. Are we ready? Right. We have a husband and a wife. We have a claim. We have food, drink, and a bedroom. All we need now are some wise women or matrons. Let's do this.

Your magic number of required wise women was five to ten, and in a city like London, these were probably all complete strangers, which might be quite unnerving, to say the least. In a small village, those wise women were potentially someone the husband was related to. Granny. Aunt Margaret. The lady next door his wife buys the eggs from on Tuesdays. Either way, this

could hardly improve performance issues he may or may not have been having.

Other times, professional women were called. The theory behind that is obvious. The women who worked in the oldest profession in the world would be the most skilled in the arts of arousing. If anyone knew what a man's glands should be doing, it's the women who see the largest amount of them on a daily basis.

The utterly thrilling thing about the bedroom trial is that the wise women were not in any way silent observers. Oh, no. They were permitted to encourage and offer advice in the form of words...

Come on John! Prove yourself a man!!

...which is pretty great if one likes a cheer squad, but a little traumatic if one doesn't. As you already know, the best modern cheer squads also have actions to accompany their cheering. As did Medieval ones. Actions. Yes.

The wise women were permitted to get hands-on with the gentleman in question. Many types of unwanted, well, we assume unwanted, physical intimacy included not only touching the husband, but rubbing his flaccid member and hitching up their own skirts and exposing their own breasts to him. We know these things are not hearsay or rumour because the court records recorded it all. Who said what. Who touched what.

I just don't know that this helped.

Alice Rassell of York

Alice Rassell was born in 1406 and had the misfortune of being trapped in an unsatisfying marriage. Literally. Maybe John wasn't a kind and loving husband or maybe Alice was more interested in someone her own age. Either way, Alice wasn't getting her share of loving and wasn't taking it lying down.

The details from the court case of John Scathelock of York, age forty, and his wife, Alice, age twenty-six, from the York church courts show exactly what happened for the unfortunate John when the trial made it past the food and drink stage and into the seclusion of a bedroom where a posse of enthusiastic women were waiting for him.

Here are some great highlights:

- July 1432 was the date and the case was recorded in Latin.
- As well as the couple, these witnesses were present and their respective ages noted:
- Joan Semer aged 40, Isabel Herwood aged 30, Joan Bank aged 26, Joan Laurence aged 36, Isabel Grymthorp aged 40, Joan Tunstall aged 36, and Margaret Bell aged 50.
- The trial took place in John Bulmer's house in Fishergate, York.
- John was stripped down to his petycote (petticote or sherte).
- John's hose and breeches were unfastened and taken down to his knees.
- John warmed himself by the fire and everyone ate and drank.
- Joan bares her breasts to John, kissed him and with her hands warmed at the fire, fondled his penis and testicles.
- Joan raised her clothes to her navel and put John's hand under her belly and told John that for shame he should display his manhood and...find out whether there was anything to please him there...and prove himself a man.
- Joan noted that John's penis was scarcely four fingers long and was...*as empty skin, having no substance to it.*

- Alice, the wife, testified she had not been known carnally by John and that she was willing and anxious to have children.
- Isabel says that John and his penis should not presume to take any wife unless he was able to please her.
- Margaret assured that everyone took turns fondling John's penis and testicles.
- Joan told that one of the women lay on a bed of straw with her bosom bared and her clothes raised to her navel and spake to John, saying he should show his manhood and gladden her heart.
- Isabel, by her own admission the most attractive of the women, although aged 40, said they raised their shins and laid upon him and they put his penis on their bare bellies.
- After consultation with the court, the Alice's marriage was dissolved on the grounds of impotence.

We have no clues as to who John Bulmer is or what his connection to the case might be, only that it was held at his house in an upstairs room. It was nice that the accused had a fire to warm up in front of before the anticipated action was due to start and also nice that one of the women warmed her hands at the fire. Cold air and frosty fingers are not a recipe for success when it comes to genitals. It would appear that at least one of the Joan's was giving him a genuine chance at a favourable outcome. The trial makes no mention of the wife Alice being present or absent, but there seemed to be a lot of touching and talk by the women.

Quite frankly, John never stood a chance.

Wife De Fonte of Canterbury

Walter de Fonte fared no better in his bedroom trail in 1292. Walter lived in Canterbury where he had to face twelve women who were described as worthy of faith, good reputation, and an honest life. Of good reputation and honest life indicate that these were not professional sex workers, but matrons of good standing in the community.

Ten Virgin Saints.

Book of Hours with Premonstratensian connections. Walters Ex Libris. Manuscript W.215, folio 68v.

The dozen stoically did their duty as witnesses and had the pleasure of informing the court afterwards that the virile member of the said Walter was useless and not the least bit virile at all. His unnamed wife was also released from her marriage.

On a side note, spare a thought for the person working at transcription for the court in those days. In pen and parchment, poised to capture in written word all the reported action or lack of it. Not surprisingly, all of the court cases which are recorded show that the husband failed to launch and the wife got her hoped-for divorce or dissolution.

The Look of Love

Now that we know what should be happening in a husband's breeches, let us turn our thoughts to the more delightful subject of personal grooming downstairs for the Medieval lady. Concerning a lady's privy parts, we know, or think we know, what's going on inside, but what do we know of what's going on outside? Was the Medieval woman trimming or going au naturel? Do we know? Do we want to know? Yes, we do. Why wouldn't we?

Griselda

We know only a little about women who chose to remain hairy down south. The tale of Griselda is a popular story originally written by Giovanni Boccaccio around 1350, and many times retold, of a cruel husband and his submissive, repressed, and enduring wife. In one version, the husband Gualtieri discusses the type of woman who, when turned out of her house in only a chemise, would *warm her wool* or *rub her pelt* against another man to procure fine clothing.

It is fairly certain that the *wool* and *pelt* referred to is the woman's pubic hair. From this we can ascertain that at least some women retained their hair.

The Miller's Wife

Geoffrey Chaucer's wife in the Miller's Tale was another woman who didn't trim down under that we know about for sure. In the story, a man named Absolon begs the miller's wife Alisoun for a kiss. She agrees, but in the dimness of the night, she presents him with not her mouth, but *hir hole*. Absolon is confused. He knows women don't have beards and yet he has just kissed one. The miller's wife, at least, was unshaven or unplucked downstairs.

If Chaucer is including information like this in his stories, writing about women being hairy downstairs, there's a good chance that it wasn't an uncommon or repulsive thing. The miller's wife wasn't a noble lady or a lady of particularly good breeding, but she was a representation of a regular woman.

Hair Removal

Body hair of any kind is a state which appears to have been mostly shunned by women of better breeding during the medieval period. Contemporary artworks, when they show the female private parts at all, show it clear of any growth of hair.

This is substantiated by at least one written account. Erasmus, in his work *In Praise of Folly*, speaks of an old woman buying herself a younger lover:

> *Nowadays any old dotard with one foot in the grave can marry a juicy young girl, even if she has no dowry... But best of all is to see the old women, almost dead and looking like skeletons who have crapt out of their graves, still mumbling "Life is sweet!" As old as they are, they are still in heat still seducing some young Phaon they have hired for large sums of money. Every day they plaster themselves with makeup and tweeze their pubic hairs; they expose their sagging breasts and try to arouse desire with their thin voices.*

Even though this text was written in 1509, it shows that at that point, it was normal for a woman to be deliberately without pubic hair. Whether this extended to the peasantry is doubtful and whether it extended to all of the European countries can only be guessed at.

Medieval tweezers made of copper alloy dated to the fourteenth century. From the Gilbert Collection.

Many books cite small tweezers made from copper alloy or silver as part of Medieval toiletry sets. Archaeological finds back this up, although we can't know for sure what was being plucked from where. Trotula de Ruggiero's eleventh-century treatise, *De Ornatu Mulierum* or *On Women's Cosmetics*, advises this hair removal remedy for women:

> *In order permanently to remove hair. Take ants' eggs, red orpiment, and gum of ivy, mix with vinegar, and rub the areas.*

Ants eggs and vinegar! That sounds delightful, doesn't it? Red orpiment might prove to be a little trickier to get hold of. Why Trotula insists on adding such exotic ingredients to her preparations is a mystery. Sure, they may work a treat, but how could the everyday woman get her hands on them? Orpiment is an orange-yellow coloured arsenic sulphide mineral which is quite likely not lying around the house and sounds a bit on the expensive side. It is found in volcanic fumaroles, hot springs, and hydrothermal veins.

Another ancient recipe from Turkey that is reputed to aid in hair removal is a paste called *rhusma*. A 1532 book of secrets includes this version which is guaranteed to work to remove or lose hair from anywhere on the body.

> *Boil together a solution of one pint of arsenic and eighth of a pint of quicklime. Go to the baths or a hot room and smear medicine over the area to be depilated. When the skin feels hot, wash quickly with hot water so the flesh doesn't come off.*

Along with your skin, if one isn't careful. Ladies, don't try that at home.

Let's suppose for a minute that a lady is suitably trimmed or not trimmed, depending on her preference, and let us turn our thoughts to cleanliness in her genital region in general before she gets sexy with her husband. Ladies these days often like to freshen up a little beforehand. Did Medieval women? Who knew?

A couple of people, apparently.

Henry de Mandeville, the Dean of Wolverhampton, who was born around 1178, had ideas about cleanliness before sex. He recommended washing the inner and outer privy members, the *pudenda*. His thoughts were that if not cleaned, the male in question might discover how old the woman might be. *Excuse* me? Discover how *old* they are? Did he suspect that older women smelled less sweet, or is he hinting that the recently virginal have a distinct smell? I guess if virgins attract unicorns by their very scent, this might have a certain wayward logic. One can only hope he kept the reason for his advice to himself.

Bathsheba at her bath, observed by King David, Bruges. Book of Hours, ca 1500.

Walters Ex Libris. Manuscript W.428, folio 132v.

Trotula, of course, also had thoughts other than her ant-related recipes for hair removal. If she didn't know for sure what *was* happening, she certainly had ideas about what *should* be happening. Ladies, grab a notepad. You'll be wanting to refer to this, and it's quite lengthy.

> *A woman before coupling should purify the inner pudenda with her fingers wrapped in dry wool. She should then carefully wipe both interior and exterior organs with a perfectly clean cloth. Next, she should part the legs widely to enable all the fluid to drain away from the interior parts. After doing so she should insert the cloth and draw the legs tightly together so as to dry them thoroughly. She should then chew the powder I have mentioned and rub her hands and breasts with it, also sprinkling rose water over the public hair, the pubes itself and all adjacent parts, for forgetting her face. She may then, thus well prepared, approach the male.*

Well, I don't know about you, but that's the most interesting pre-sex advice I've heard since the Karma Sutra suggested I become a master at laying floor tiles in an effort to win the heart of the man I most admire. Not adhering to advice like this is probably why I'm single. I mean, not once have I drained all the fluid away from my interior parts akin to having a grease and oil change or personally chewed the powder I've failed to rub my breasts with. Clearly, my approaching-of-the-male technique might be improved.

If you aren't doing any of these things, you might like to take a good look at yourself and readjust your wooing technique also.

Chapter 6

Sexy Foods and How to Have Them

If a lady felt her husband was able enough but not willing enough, she could try to increase his libido with herbal remedies and enticing foods. Today when we think of sexy food, we think of chocolate-dipped strawberries, oysters, and herbal supplements like ginseng, ginkgo biloba, or horny goatweed guaranteed to enflame desire.

There are others that we avoid. The general consensus on garlic bread these days is that it is a bit of a passion-killer unless eaten by both parties. I can see you nodding from here.

Aphrodisiacs

Arousing desire in either a reluctant lover or one whose virile member isn't up to the task is as much of an issue today as it was to the Medieval woman. What a lady needed was a little something to set the scene gastronomically.

We all know that the way to a man's heart is through his stomach, but it's also felt that the way to a man's groin might be gained in the same way. Giving a man delicious homecooked foods and baked treats is a sure-fire way to get him thinking fondly of you. Nothing fires up lust faster than a good aphrodisiac, but did the Medieval woman take this approach also? She certainly did. The most recommended aphrodisiacs were libido-enhancers in the form of food or herbals. These might be taken internally or externally or, sometimes, both.

Sounds intriguing, doesn't it?

We've already learned from the questions asked in the confessional that baked vagina-smothered fish might be helpful.

If that wasn't rousing the passions fast enough, a good alternate aphrodisiac may do the trick. Trotula's helpful books offered suggestions for improving a woman's sex life, as did Hildegarde von Bingen's. They were definitely the two go-to girls of the time.

One might mistakenly think that potions, charms, and aphrodisiacs were not sanctioned by the church, and in some cases, that was true. Happily, in other cases, they thought more scientifically. Apparently, logic taught that since God had provided the fruits in the fields, it was His intention that they be used to aid mankind. Even the women. They were a kind of *natural* magic. As long as the herbals were used with the correct amount of reverence and the proper kind of prayer, God would approve. And if they didn't work, it was because He willed it and it was definitely also a part of his plan. There was a fine line between God's natural bounty and witchcraft, so pay attention.

herbs for her

That a woman might need to increase her sexual desire was quite a laughable idea.

herbs for him

Herbals could be procured almost anywhere. Most villages had cottage gardens, and this is where the country girl had the advantage over her city sister. Town gardens were limited to essentials, whereas the country garden had access to fresh air, compost, and the room to grow a larger variety of plants.

Let's take a look at some of the more common ones that could easily be added to a meal as a tasty and sexy stimulant. Hildegard starts out with arnica.

> ***Arnica**: is very hot and has a poisonous heat in it. If a person's skin has been touched with fresh arnica, he or she will burn lustily with love for the person who is afterward touched by the same herb. He or she will be so incensed with love, almost infatuated, and will become a fool.*

Well, that sounds promising! Incensed! Infatuated! Yes! That should lead to intercourse, yes? Sprinkle that stuff on and cross your fingers! Should arnica not be available or just not produce the desired results, she recommends mascel.

> ***Mascel**: The mascel has a useless and harmful heat and its wood, sap and leaves are harmful to his health and is dangerous for his libido, since it excites lust in a person. If a person eats its fruit, he will become sick with it. Its fire and smoke are not good for a person's health.*

Strictly speaking, mascel is a type of tree, not an herb, but it's not a fruit either, or a food. Don't smoke it. Or eat the fruit. Noted. Instructions on what to do with the wood, sap, and leaves would have been great for the inciting of the lusting, but they are mysteriously absent.

Further herbals can be found in the widely distributed heath manuals like the *Tacuinum Sanitatis,* and they have the added benefit of mentioning whether there are dangers linked to taking the herb and what to do about them. This remedy comes from the Vienna copy.

Nasturtiums were extremely helpful to encourage both coitus and sperm.

> **Garden nasturtiums**, *(eruca et nasturtium)*
>
> **Nature**: *Warm and humid in the first degree.*
>
> **Optimum:** *Those which have the best flavour.*
>
> **Usefulness:** *Augment the sperm and coitus.*
>
> **Dangers:** *Cause migraines.*

Neutralisation of the dangers: *With a salad of escarole and vinegar.*

Nasturtiums appear very useful not only to increase the sex drive, but to increase sperm—rather important if one is desiring a pregnancy. You may well have many of these in your own garden or growing potted in a sunny spot on your kitchen windowsill. Nevertheless, don't try these at home.

Sexy Foods for Her

As I've already mentioned, the woman needs no amount of libido lifting. They *are* the lusty ones. Pay attention and try to keep up.

Sexy Foods for Him

The Medieval woman had a great deal of advice available to her in the form of foods she might like to try for various ailments or, in this instance, lack of libido. Most of them came with quite specific instructions on the best times to eat them and helpfully included any unwanted side effects and how to avoid them.

Herbal Handbooks

One of the best known and most copied herbal texts in the Medieval world was the *Tacuinum Sanitatus*, a health book dealing with the properties and usefulness of medicinal herbs, plants, foods, and clothing. Each singular page includes a large, gloriously coloured illumination depicting the item with its name and properties below. Some were copied verbatim, but the *Tacuinum Sanitatus of Vienna* otherwise known as *The Four Seasons of the House of Cerruti* also noted foods which were not eaten locally, like bananas, and carefully listed what the current thoughts were about them. There are five copies still existing from the fourteenth and early fifteenth centuries, and the text was widely accepted as an authority on all important life matters. It's in this book, also, that we find *coitus* illustrated, showing the

missionary position for those who aren't sure how to have coitus and describing its health benefits.

Oysters were definitely not a food to be recommended. They were found on rocks at the bottom of waterbodies and were a bit unclean. Most of the other things found in rivers or in the sea swam above the bottom of the beds and higher up in the water and were less polluted. Oysters were not recommended, period, let alone recommended as an aphrodisiac. Luckily, the book does have other ideas.

These helpful suggestions for promoting better sex with foods included:

> ***Bananas*** *(musse). We know of it only from texts or tales from the merchants from Cyprus or the Holy Land. Sicilians, on the other hand, know them well. The leaves are fan shaped and have a hard rib and a thin blade which dries up in the summer. The banana has a yellow skin when ripe and white pulp. It seems at first to be very insipid-tasting, but then they say one can never eat enough of them due to their delicious flavour which gradually emerges very pleasantly. They weigh heavily on the stomach and their only virtue is that they are sexually arousing.*

Arousing, you say? Bananas? Who knew!

In this case, the banana was clearly not a food which was accessible to the everyday housewife. She needed to look more towards things she may have in her own garden. Leeks? Might she have leeks?

> ***Houseleek:*** *Houseleek is cold and not beneficial to eat because of the richness of its nature. If a man who is healthy in his genital nature should eat it, he would be totally on fire with lust and he would become as if crazy.*

On fire with lust. Okay, that's more like it!

You may not have much of a garden if you live in an inner-city unit or apartment, but that's certainly something to keep in mind the next time you go shopping. Put that chocolate body paint right back on the shelf and make a beeline for the fresh produce department. Try not to look suspicious if you're loading up your trolley with more than one bunch. Leeks. Great!

What else might the hopeful Medieval woman try? If leeks sound a little doubtful, you may not be keen on the next suggestion either. Onions. Onions will help facilitate coitus. Apparently. Leeks *and* onions. It's a dynamite pairing. I'll bet the Medieval woman couldn't believe her luck at that wonderful piece of advice. Onions are super sexy, right? Let's check out what it says:

> ***Onions*** *(cepe)*
>
> ***Nature:*** *Warm in the fourth degree, moist in the third degree.*
>
> ***Optimum:*** *The white ones which are watery and juicy.*
>
> ***Usefulness:*** *They are diuretic and facilitate coitus.*
>
> ***Dangers:*** *They cause headaches.*
>
> ***Neutralisation of dangers:*** *With vinegar and milk.*

Looking at that, leek and onion soup sounds like a safe bet for a good time in, though the chances of having breath that could strip paint off walls seems likely. The best onions, of course, are the juicy white ones, but if those aren't available, certainly any kind of onion might do. They just may not be quite as effective.

It seems that headaches may be a problem, though that really may have been a fake excuse to get away from the onion breath. It's extremely helpful to know that milk and vinegar will help with the headaches, but it's less helpful in that it doesn't say how.

Cook the onion in vinegar and then drink the milk? Simmer the onion in milk and add a vinegar drizzle dressing? Boil the whole lot up into a kind of soupy glue? Eat the onion raw, chug some vinegar, and follow with a milk chaser? Drink the milk first to

line the stomach for the vinegary onion that is to follow and just hope for the best? Those leeks are looking pretty reasonable now, aren't they? I thought so.

If one couldn't get exotics like bananas or didn't fancy onion breath, perhaps the answer lay in your own chicken coop. Eggs. Try some sexy, sexy eggs. Still reading in the same health handbook, we read that the properties of eggs were these:

> ***Chicken eggs*** *(ou a galinearum)*
>
> ***Nature:*** *The albumen is cold and moist, the yolk is warm and moist.*
>
> ***Optimum:*** *Those which are fresh and large.*
>
> ***Usefulness:*** *They increase coitus noticeably.*
>
> ***Dangers:*** *They slow down digestion and cause freckles.*
>
> ***Neutralisation of the dangers:*** *By eating only the yolk.*

Honestly! How was this decided? To counteract the bad digestion whilst getting more sex and less freckles, eat only the yolk? In a medical publication of this widespread popularity, there ought to be proven remedies, not wild guesses. Exactly how many people ate just the yolk and how many ate the entire egg? What percentage of these were less freckled as a result? I'm really keen to know. Looking at the eggs, milk, onion, and leeks, why not just combine all four ingredients and make a super-delicious omelette or scrambled eggs?

Onion breath and flatulence from the eggs just doesn't sound all that lusty to me. Gusty, but not lusty. One last food one might also have considered is chestnuts, which have the added benefit of being nourishing as well as being favourable to coitus. Once again, they were dangerously likely to cause headaches. Typical.

Meats for her

Oh, seriously? I'll spell it out for you one last time. The lady does not need inflaming. She is a hotbed of repressed, sexual frenzy just waiting for it. The lady does not need the meat.

No snickering now.

Meats for him

If herbs, fruits, and vegetables aren't making an impression in the underpants area, the Medieval woman might like to try something else guaranteed to get his mouth watering...meat! Hildegard's book *Physica* lists a number of meats expected to bring lust back into the bedroom if fed to the reluctant man. The most obvious choice is bear. Definitely, a lady should try to get her hands on some bear meat.

According to Hildegard, this should be the result:

> ***Bear:*** *If it is eaten, it will so fire up lust in a person...*

Marginalia bear.

King David penitent, Hours of Duke Adolph of Cleves, Walters Ex Libris, Manuscript W.439, folio 204v.

I would imagine the sheer acquisition of actual bear might fire up a certain amount of lustful admiration from the reluctant gentleman friend. Let's consider that this treatise came from a German woman and a nun. Exactly how this advice came to her is perplexing. It's unlikely that her town was overrun with bears or that there was an abundance of bear meat in the marketplaces or that it was the latest fad diet.

The Medieval German cookbook *Ein Buch von guter Spice* is the earliest known recipe book dating between 1345 to 1354. It fails to mention bear meat at all. Shockingly, or not, James Matterer's *A Boke of Gode Cookery*, which is a modern compilation of over a hundred authentic Medieval recipes, is likewise devoid of bear.

If bear meat is scarce at the local deli, and I honestly suspect it may be, perhaps a woman should try to woo her disinterested man with pork, which at least has a certain wordplay associated to it these days. Whether it did back then seems unlikely, but a woman might try to pork her husband in the hope of these results:

> ***Pig:*** *They create lust in a person, with a force that would make a wheel roll, and they render him unclean in another way.*

A force that would make a wheel roll? That takes some thinking about. What kind of wheel? How big was the wheel? Was the force measured perchance? What was the acceleration of the wheel and was it on an even surface, so the measurements were not impaired?

On the subject of pigs, how are pigs expected to make a man less clean than he already was? There are so many questions. Some of these slightly more exotic foodstuffs might be harder to get hold of today, so maybe just skip them and make do with oysters. Or chocolate.

The burning question is—did any of these recipes *actually* work? Did they?

Asking for a friend.

Chapter 7

How to Get Pregnant

Babymakers

Producing an heir was serious business for the Medieval family, and a new bride was expected to provide a male heir to keep the family name, business, and land holdings. A marriage was not deemed proper or legally binding until coitus had taken place, usually with witnesses.

Not surprisingly, there was much advice written on the best times for procreation to produce male heirs, which were the best kind of heirs to have, along with many recipes to guarantee a pregnancy or to help it along—some more bizarre than others. On the whole, it was not a good idea to leave these things to chance when a hopeful mum-to-be could enhance her chances.

Virgin and Child. Early fourteenth century. German Homilary from the Walters Ex Libris. W.148 folio 63r.

Conception

Medieval medicine was reasonably advanced in some ideas and, yet, not others. The basic understanding of how conception occurred was known since the ancient Greeks and Romans and

long before the text attributed to Magnus in thirteenth-century Europe was circulated.

The *De secretis mulierum* or *Secrets of Women* had much written about the workings of women's bodies, including how babies were formed. Conception happened when both seeds were emitted and the situation was consenting. The male seed must be joined with the female seed through intercourse. The seeds mingle together within the woman, and then:

> *...the womb closes up like a purse on every side, so that nothing can fall out of it. After this happens, the woman no longer menstruates.*

So, the basic understanding of how it happened was there, even if some of the specifics were sketchy. His seed went in and mingled with her seed and the whole thing sealed itself off so the foetus wouldn't fall out. More or less.

Excellent.

Before we delve into giving the Medieval woman the best chance she had of gaining a successful pregnancy, other things need to be considered. Clearly, the day needed to be considered. The time of day. The intended partner. The moment in her menstrual cycle. The location of the proposed tryst. The position she might like to try. The choice of alluring headwear. And the sex needed to be consenting by both parties.

It was a well-known fact that un-consensual sex could not lead to pregnancy, something which made proving rape extremely difficult. If a woman had become pregnant as a result of unwilling sex, the fact that she had fallen pregnant proved that she was actually quite willing and just lying about being forced. No, really.

Once these things were checked off or roundly ignored in favour of reckless spontaneous lovemaking, there were still further things to consider. Especially if one was hoping for a child of a

specific gender as an outcome. It wasn't good enough to leave that to chance, either.

Gendering Assistance

Our female medic Trotula de Ruggiero, she of the *Women's Complaints*, had a great deal of useful and sometimes unusual advice for conceiving a child. She took it one step further in her thoughts for pregnancy by giving specific recipes for specific gender outcomes, which was extremely useful if one desperately needed a male heir and looked like they were to be replaced for failing to provide one.

For a Boy

Trotula advises this to conceive a male child:

> *If she wishes to conceive a male, let her husband take the womb and vagina of a hare and let him dry them, and let him mix the powder with wine and drink it.*

Ew. She completely fails to mention where to get the womb of a hare from and one assumes it's just leftovers from any dish requiring a rabbit. The wine seems like a great idea. She doesn't specify how much wine, but if it's to disguise the flavour of powdered womb, I'd suggest as much as can be bought for the occasion.

I'm rather impressed that in order for the woman to produce a male child, *he* is the one doing the preparation and the drinking. Nice work there, Trotula.

For a Girl

Girls weren't the obvious choice when it came to babies. Inheritance might be tricky if there were siblings and a suitable dowry provided if the hopes were for a suitable marriage.

Nevertheless, should a mother-to-be particularly desire to conceive a female child, Trotula offers this advice:

> *Similarly, let the woman do the same thing with the testicles of a hare and at the end of her period let her lie with her husband and then she will conceive a male.*

If one was hoping for sugar and spice and everything nice, it's a bit of a disappointment to read the ingredients list. Testicles are not even a little bit sugary or the least bit spicy. It *is* interesting to note that for a male child, the womb is used and is drunk by the husband and for a female child, the testicles are used and drunk by the wife.

No special reason is given for this. Opposites attract?

Inability to Conceive

Choosing a gender was well and good if falling pregnant in the first place wasn't a problem. For a woman unable to conceive, Trotula also had few terrific remedies to recommend which also involved sexy, sexy offal. This might be given to either the husband or the wife, depending on where the fault lay.

> *Take the liver and testicles of a small pig which is the only one a sow has borne, and let these be dried and reduced to a powder, and let it be given in a potion to a male who is not able to generate and he will generate or to a woman and she will conceive.*

Mmmm, testicle breath. If that seems a little too specific or the lineage or the size of the small pig is in question, another almost identical recipe is offered aimed at the woman who was having trouble. More offal was required. It's almost as if she was getting a kickback from the butcher who supplied these things.

> *If the woman wishes to become pregnant, take the testicles of an uncastrated male pig or wild boar and dry them and let a powder be made, and let her drink this with wine after purgation of the menses. The let her cohabit with her husband and she will conceive.*

Trotula states categorically that one must use the testicles of an *uncastrated* male pig, but to the best of my knowledge, a castrated one doesn't *have* any testicles to use, so it seems quite redundant to be that specific about the pig. They don't just grow back. The powdered preparation is to be given in wine, and not just *a potion*, which seems like a good move. It would definitely help with the testicle breath, which might be putting the husband off.

She doesn't stop there. Ladies, here is another one for you. You'll need a nice ass for this one.

> *In another fashion, let the woman take damp wool dipped in ass's milk and let her tie it upon her navel and let it stay there until she has intercourse.*

Stale milk is sexy, right? Said no nursing mother ever.

Let's now assume that the woman is sufficiently wined and dined on the appropriate preparation of testicles from the correct animals. Still not conceiving? Perhaps it's not her. Perhaps it's him. Should the lack of conception lay in the fault of the husband, with the sex act going adequately well, but no emission taking place, Hildegard stepped up with a hot tip to assist. Of course, she did. Why wouldn't she?

> *If a man is stirred up in delight, so that his sperm arrives at the point of emission but has in some way been retained in his body and he has begun to be ill from it, he should take rue and a bit less wormwood, add a greater amount of bear fat, and pound these together. He should vigorously rub*

> *himself with it, around his kidneys and loins, whilst near a fire.*

Bear fat? *Bear* fat! Smear some bear fat and rub your loins! I feel the vigorous rubbing of the loins will definitely help with emissions, but I'm a bit less confident about the bear fat. And if that doesn't help, the wormwood will keep the fleas away for a bit, so that's nice.

If he is perhaps having trouble for another reason, a woman might try either of these two amazing cures for better semen which should lead to a sure-fire pregnancy. It's back to the garden for the first one. Remember that lust-inducing houseleek? Happily, it will do more than just get his engine revving, although as a chaste woman, I'm certain that Hildegard was working on hearsay and not personal experience. She advises:

> ***Houseleek:*** *And if any man is dried up in his semen because his semen is deficient from old age, let him place houseleek in goat's milk long enough for it to be drenched in all the milk. Then he should cook it with the same milk, with a few eggs added so that it can be food. Then he should eat it for three or five days. His semen will receive the powers of begetting, and will flourish for the purposes of offspring. Food this way is not useful for female sterility.*

It may or may not be helpful, but it is almost a recipe for an omelette or scrambled eggs, so it sounds far tastier than many of the others. Unlike any of the testicle-or-womb recipes, a woman may at least have a chance to get him to eat it.

The next semen-enhancing preparation she might entice her husband with was herbal. If he wasn't keen on eggs, why not try hazel? You'll also need a goat for this one. I kid you not.

> ***Hazel:*** *The hazel tree is more cold than hot and is not much good for medicine. It symbolises lasciviousness. A*

male whose semen has diffuse quality, so that it does not engender offspring, should take large hazelnuts, a third as much smartweed, and a quarter as much bindweed as smartweed. He should cook this with some pepper and the liver of a young he-goat which is old enough to procreate. Then he should add it to a little raw, fatty pork meat. He should also dip bread in the water in which this meat was cooked, and eat it. If he does this often, he will flourish with progeny, if the righteous judgement of God does not prohibit it.

The hazel recipe makes the egg-and-leek combo look positively scrumptious.

It was entirely possible that even with these fabulous recipes for pregnancy, which were almost certain to succeed, the very usual disclaimer *unless God does not will it* usually applied. Not because one had the wrong kind of wine or whether or not your pig was delivered from the right kind of sow.

That would be crazy talk.

To Combat Sterility

If a woman seemed truly sterile, was there hope for her? Why are you asking? There was always hope. Hopes and prayers. Failing that, there was always our dynamic duo, Trotula and Hildegard. First, before the finger-pointing and name-calling started, it should be determined which of the two parties was the sterile one. Maybe it wasn't her. Maybe it was him? Who could tell? Happily, there was a simple test for this, too. All you'd need was two pots and a quantity of bran. Then, proceed as follows:

Take two pots and in each one place bran and put some of the man's urine in one of them with the bran and in the other, some urine of the woman and let the pots sit for nine or ten days. If the infertility is the fault of the woman, you

> *will find many worms in her pot and the bran will stink. In the other, if it is the man's fault. And if you find this in neither, then in neither is there any defect and they are able to be aided by the benefit of medicine so that they might conceive.*

I could be mistaken, but it seems to me like a perfectly good waste of bran.

Confirming a Pregnancy

If one was not sure whether conception had occurred and the child was too young to be active in the womb, a Medieval woman might consult a doctor for confirmation by testing her urine.

Urology was a thriving science in the Middle Ages, and many hours were devoted to the study of the analysis of urine. *The Seeing of the Urine* was a text devoted to the signs and signals which were expected to be seen as a direct result of any number of medical conditions.

The doctor would check the urine for its colour and its clarity, or in the case of some illnesses, check its taste. He would then consult with his textbooks for a diagnosis. Thankfully, when it came to verifying pregnancy, a visual was enough. He could be quite certain of that:

> *Urine of a woman red as gold with a watery circle above betokens that she is with child.*

Or, if clear urine doesn't seem to be working for you, it might be clear, but not altogether clear.

> *Urine of women that be with child, the water shall have some clear strikes, the most part shall be troubled, and the troubledness shall be reddish, in the manner of tawny, and this token shall never fail.*

Troubledness, you say? Build a bridge and get over it. This seems to be consistent with almost everything we know about Medieval urology. It's definitely one thing. Unless it's the other thing. Either way, it was definitely one of them. Unless it was the other thing.

If a woman was expecting a child and wished to know what sex one might be having, the urine might be further consulted to find out. It took an expert to determine these things, and not every doctor was able to read the signs and make a correct diagnosis. The way to correctly gender a babe in the womb was this:

> *As soon as the child has life, and it be a girl, the troubledness shall be draw downwards, and if it be a boy, the troubledness shall have above.*

No clues were given for what the troubledness actually was, but it was certain that the peculiarities of this were known to the medic who was doing the investigating. It was a skill and a fine art. Cloudy with a chance of clear sounds more like a weather forecast than science, but words used to describe the temperaments of women have often been referred to this way. A mild countenance. A fair complexion. Why should her urine be any different?

A doctor examines a urine flask. 1315–1325.

Psalter Hours, Ghent. Walters Ex Libris. W.82. folio75v.

What any pregnant mother-to-be didn't wish to see was white urine, which indicated something was not going well for either her baby, herself, or both:

Urine of a woman coloured as is white lead, if she be with child, it betokens that the child is dead within her. And if she not be with child and the water stink, it betokens that the mother is rotten.

Either way, it was bad news.

If a woman didn't fancy checking out her urine, she might be able to sex her child within the uterus by just looking at herself or examining the way she moved. Bartholomew the Englishman wrote:

The mother suffers less from the conception of a boy child and her colouring is therefore more beautiful and cleaner, and her movements lighter than during the conception of a girl as Aristotle and Constantine say. It is a sign of impregnation that the mothers desire different things, the colouring changes, the area under the eyes turns black, the breasts are enlarged, and the uterus grows slowly in size. Because of the size of the growing foetus, she suffers nausea and vomiting, feels heavy and unable to work.

Once a pregnancy was confirmed, what might the first-time mother-to-be look forward to as far as her confinement goes? On the whole, everything known to women about pregnancy could be summed up in one word: suffering. If there was a pregnancy, expect a whole heap of extensive suffering.

A treatise on virginity called *Holy Maidenhood* was particularly descriptive and gave a lengthy account of what to expect when you're expecting. It was written near Herefordshire, in England, sometime between 1180 and 1210, but by whom is unsure. We can be sure that whoever wrote it had definitely seen morning sickness up close when they wrote:

Your rosy face will grow thin and turn green as grass; your eyes will grow dull, and shadowed underneath, and because

> *of your dizziness your head will ache cruelly. Inside, in your belly, a swelling in your womb which bulges you out like a water-skin, discomfort in your bowels and stitches in your side, and often painful backache; heaviness in every limb; the dragging weight of your two breasts, and the streams of milk that run from them. Your beauty is all destroyed by pallor; there is a bitter taste in your mouth, and everything that you eat makes you feel sick; and whatever food your stomach disdainfully receives—that is, with distaste—it throws up again.*

That sounds positively delightful, doesn't it? And if that wasn't enough to put you off altogether, there's more. Not content to describe what a hideous thing a woman becomes when she's with child, there is the matter of the actual birth to contend with.

The treatise continues with as much comfort as before:

> *Worry about your labour pains keeps you awake at night. Then when it comes to it, that cruel distressing anguish, that fierce and stabbing pain, that incessant misery, that torment upon torment, that wailing outcry; whilst you are suffering from this and from your fear of death, shame added to that suffering with that shameful craft of old wives who know about that painful ordeal, whose help is necessary to you, however indecent it may be; and there you must put up with whatever happens to you.*

So much for the precious joys and the wonder of nature and the joyful glow of impending motherhood.

The accuracy of the description, whilst being graphic and harsh, is surprisingly accurate and detailed. Most women who have faced a pregnancy can recognise most of those symptoms—dark circles under the eyes from sleeping poorly when heavily pregnant, cravings, nausea and vomiting, and waddling like a hippo.

Some things change, some stay the same.

Pregnancy Dos and Don'ts

Taking some time for self-care was tricky for a lady at this time. She couldn't just lie around for nine months taking it easy when there was so much to do. Anglo-Saxon medical texts had advice for the expectant mother. There was not a great deal about what she should do, but quite a lengthy list of things she shouldn't.

In the *Leechbook III* by Bald, we find this:

> *A pregnant woman is to be earnestly warned that she should eat nothing salty or sweet, or drink beer, or eat swine's flesh or anything fat, or drink to intoxication, or travel by road, or ride too much by horseback, lest the child be born before the proper time.*

On the whole, these are pretty solid suggestion for the expectant mother, and most of which are good advice still today. Regarding the sweet or salty foods, a mother may have cravings, but she may prefer plain food if she has an unsettled stomach. The recommendations avoiding alcohol are still relevant, as is the comment about horse riding. All in all, as far as historical advice for pregnant women goes, it's pretty good.

There were some things she could try to make her situation more comfortable. Some herbs and foods might provide a little relief from morning sickness if she was wise enough to seek them out. Modern women might also try herbal teas, but what might the Medieval woman try?

Nausea Remedies

A woman suffering from the nausea of morning sickness was doing so because she was descended from Eve, let's just remember that. No remedy was needed for morning sickness.

If one was determined to go against the natural order of things and hope to take something to feel better, a woman might try fresh leaves of the plant woodruff *asperula odorata*, made into tea and drunk. She might also try some recommendations from the handbook, the *Tacuinum Sanitatus*, which weren't specifically directed towards pregnant women, but may have addressed their symptoms.

The Rouen version suggests candied orange peel, which sounds a bit delightful if one was rich enough to import it or lived in a European country that grew orange trees.

> ***Oranges*** *(cetrona id est narancia)*
>
> ***Nature:*** *The pulp is cold and humid in the third degree, the skin is dry and warm in the second.*
>
> ***Optimum:*** *Those that are perfectly ripe.*
>
> ***Usefulness:*** *Their candied skin is good for the stomach.*
>
> ***Dangers:*** *They are difficult to digest.*
>
> ***Neutralisation of the dangers:*** *Accompanied by the best wine.*

Or how about violets?

> ***Violets*** *(viole)*
>
> ***Nature:*** *Cold in the first degree, humid in the second.*
>
> ***Optimum:*** *Lapis-lazuli coloured, with many leaves.*
>
> ***Usefulness:*** *When smelled they calm frenzies, when drunk they purify bilious humours.*
>
> ***Dangers:*** *They are bad for catarrh caused by the cold.*
>
> ***Effects:*** *None. They are suitable for warm and dry temperaments, for young people, in Summer, and in the Southerly region.*

Next time you're feeling poorly, you might like to try those last two. I'm pretty partial to some candied orange peel, and who isn't cheered by a bunch of violets to sniff? Frenzy-calming seems like a bit of a stretch, but one supposes it depends on the level of the frenzy one is experiencing.

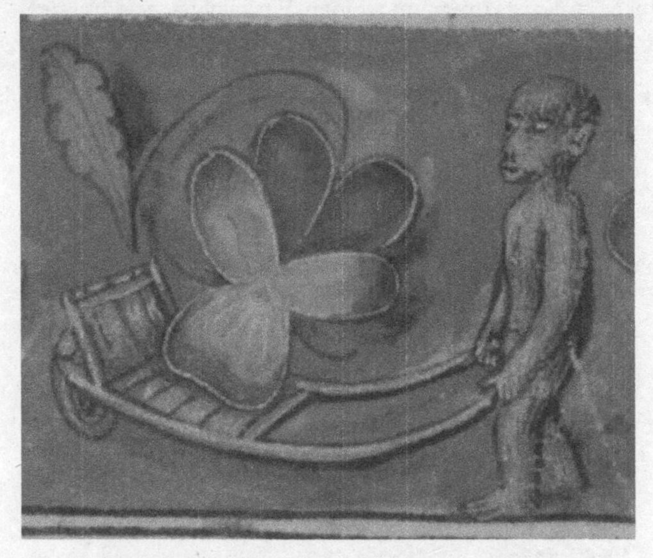

Marginalia monkey with wheelbarrow and violet.

Initial "O" with manuscript owner Adolph of Cleves revering the Virgin of Humility and Child, Hours of Duke Adolph of Cleves, Walters Ex Libris. Manuscript W.439, folio 80v.

Spilt some milk? Smell those violets! Cat hacked up a hairball on your work clothes before work? Smell those violets! Toddler throwing a tantrum? Breathe them right in deeply whilst counting to ten under your breath. Pouty teenager shrieking incoherently whilst attempting to leave the house *dressed like that* whilst husband asks what's for dinner whilst you burn yourself on the iron and get a text message that your credit card has been declined on your electricity bill and you will be without power in less than an hour? I won't lie to you. Violets may not help you here unless you are extremely proactive.

Try leaving the house and driving immediately to the nearest nursery and buying all the violets in stock. Put them in your car.

Spending time amongst flowers is particularly good for the soul, especially if you leave the rest of the family at home and your car is now a cloud of perfume. Treat yourself to take-away on the way home. See? It did help, after all.

Difficult Confinements

Should a pregnancy prove to be troublesome or the birth itself look like it was likely to be difficult, might there be some assistance available? Naturally, there was; it just wasn't very practical.

It required a large amount of prayers, and, if one was extremely fortunate, a physical object to wear in the form of a birthing girdle. The term girdle refers not to what we consider today to be a girdle—that is, a restrictive tummy-flattener—but a belt, the same kind as any other regular belt. Birthing girdles were thought to have miraculous powers of relief which were psychosomatic at best.

Noble ladies who lived in the right part of the country might loan the virgin's girdle supposedly worn by the Virgin Mary herself when she gave birth, but others had to settle for a regular one which had been blessed or perhaps sprinkled with holy water. At Rievaulx Abbey in Yorkshire, monks guarded the girdle of St Ailred as it was known to be helpful to ladies lying in. One assumed it was available to those who were good and devout women, meaning those who made large donations to the church on a regular basis. Because they were precious and a bit mystical, girdles might be handed down in the family with reverence and care, and we find one mentioned in an English will dated 1508:

> *Also, one small girdle harnessed with silver and gilt, which is an heirloom, called Our Lady's Girdle, for sick women with child. I will that it be delivered to my son Roger, to remain as an heirloom.*

In this record, it is noted that the girdle is extremely valuable with expensive gilt fittings and is being given to Roger, presumably for his wife or future wife. This may indicate a couple of different things. Either Roger had no sisters to leave the belt to or it was far too valuable to leave the girdle to a mere woman when the bloodline was clearly the responsibility of Roger and his heirs. The safe delivery of his offspring was more important than the babies of daughters who were providing the future generations of someone else's family. It may be that Roger had no sisters at all and that the girdle was given to him only because of a lack of them, but I suspect not. It was also made quite clear that the girdle was to remain in the family.

Many options were available for the woman who was birthing, but none were particularly effective. Largely, these consisted of herbal poultices, folk remedies, and devout prayer. Invoking the name of Saint Margaret, the patron saint of childbirth, was always believed to ease labour pains and assure a safe delivery.

St Margaret issuing from dragon.

Book of Hours with Premonstratensian connections, Walters Ex Libris. Manuscript W.215, folio 67r.

Potions advocated for childbirth in the Middle Ages included rubbing the flanks of the expectant mother with rose oil, giving her vinegar and sugar to drink, or applying poultices of ivory or eagle's dung.

Gemstones were also utilised to ease childbirth, but how they were anything other than a placebo is a mystery. Placing a magnet in the mother's hand was believed to provide relief. If that didn't work, she might try wearing coral around her neck. In the twelfth century, Hildegard von Bingen wrote of the powers of the stone called sard:

> *If a pregnant woman is beset by pain but is unable to give birth, rub sard around both of her thighs and say "Just as you, stone, by the order of God, shone on the first angel, so you, child, come forth a shining person, who dwells with God." Immediately, hold the stone at the exit for the child, that is, the female member, and say, "Open you roads and door, in that epiphany by which Christ appeared both human and God, and opened the gates of Hell. Just so, child, may you also come out of this door without dying, and without the death of your mother." Then tie the same stone to a belt and cinch it around her, and she will be cured.*

Or not. Another suggestion for the delivery of a breech birth said that the midwife should do this:

> *...with her small and gentle hand moistened with a decoction of flaxseed and chickpeas, put the child back in its place and proper position.*

Which at least sounds quite useful and extremely practical. Not too sure about those chickpeas, though.

Breastfeeding

Post-natal care was not a particularly widespread phenomenon in the Middle Ages. A certain amount of care was required to deal with the new mother's recovering body, but even medicine had some unusual ideas about it.

The breast milk from a newly-birthing mother contained the remains of the blood from the womb, it was thought. The blood turned white as it was purified through the bosom to expel as white breast milk. This being so, it stood to reason that any character flaws or family traits would also be passed on to the child in this way.

Wet Nurses

Wet nurses were extremely popular amongst the upper classes who were far too busy to suckle their own children, so before hiring a servant who might provide milk to a baby, it was crucial the servant be checked for defects in her physical self as well as her moral stance and general countenance. Milk from a woman who did not possess good qualities herself was without a doubt going to pass them onto the unfortunate baby.

Thomas of Chobham, the Arch-deacon we met earlier who had very little to say kindly to women, was extremely down on mothers who did not breastfeed their own children. In his eyes, he considered it a sin on a par with murder because no other milk could be more suitable for a baby than the one God had provided, and to reject God's gift was inexcusable.

Should a woman claim that she was too delicate to manage the feeding herself, Thomas sermonised sternly, saying the she certainly didn't seem too delicate to have sex and conceive. If the birth had been difficult, he also felt that feeding the baby and bathing it herself was the very least she could do.

Maternity Wear

Special clothing for breastfeeding was not an option for the poorer woman who could not afford to extend her wardrobe for the sake of pregnancy. Feeding was usually achieved by undoing the kirtle at the front and pulling the chemise or smock down also.

The Virgin breastfeeding.

Hours of Duke Adolph of Cleaves. Walters Ex Libris. W.439 folio14r.

Some paintings from the high medieval period which feature the baby Jesus show Mary wearing a gown which either has a buttoned flap at the front to allow her to access her breasts, or a garment with two concealed, vertical slits at chest level which are used to pop the breast through for super-convenient feeding access. Whilst, in theory, this would work extremely well, the question of how the breast gets through the linen undergarment is perplexing.

Post-Natal Depression

Women were noted to sometimes suffer from what was known as melancholia, which was an unexplained sadness brought on for no apparent reason other than an imbalance of bile in the humours. Hippocrates, however, noticed that this sadness sometimes coincided with a woman who had recently given birth and, in the fourth century BC, suggested that there might be a link.

His theory, which was adopted by many forward-thinking medical men right through until the Middle Ages, was that if

the fluid that came from the woman's uterus after the birth of a child did not drain correctly and was somehow suppressed, it might flow back up to the head and cause untold issues including delirium, mania, and agitation.

We call it postpartum depression today, and we know for sure that the symptoms are a medical actuality, even if Hippocrates didn't quite understand the cause correctly. He knew something was going on and had come close to the cause-and-effect correlation. He had the effect part right.

Trotula also had ideas. She also blamed the moistures in a woman's body post-birth to be the root of the trouble but was a bit more general in specifying what they were, simply calling it excess moisture. She helpfully wrote:

> *If the womb is too moist, the brain is filled with water, and the moisture running over the eyes, compels them to involuntarily shed tears.*

I don't think one needs a lot of Medieval training to notice that new mothers seem tired, stressed, and weepy. This might be managed with good foods or other remedies, which sometimes might include bathing or pilgrimage. Giving thanks for a safe delivery was also a smashing reason to go on pilgrimage, so it seems legitimate, if not wildly impractical.

At the very least, sex should be avoided for a month after the baby's birth.

Chapter 8

How to Be Not Pregnant

That's all rather well if you wanted a baby, but what if you didn't? Perhaps you had too many mouths to feed already. Perhaps you were a woman of delicate constitution and just weren't up for being pregnant all the time. Perhaps you just didn't like your husband overmuch?

Was there anything the Medieval woman could do about not having babies? Surely something could be done? Indeed, there was. A number of somethings.

Thoughts and Prayers

Nothing works better than thoughts and prayers, right? Oh. It doesn't? It's certainly worth a shot if one isn't too fussed on whether it works or not. Praying to not get pregnant was something women did, but even an unshakable faith in the Lord will not actively prevent pregnancy.

Marginalia woman praying.

Book of Hours. Walters Ex Libris. W.90. folio 135v. France, early fourteenth century.

Thoughts and prayers weren't particularly recommended anyway, since a woman was only having sex hoping to conceive, remember. Why would she want to have sex otherwise? Okay, let's look at some options for the Medieval woman hell-bent on thwarting what was potentially going to happen if she got sexy.

Abstinence

Just Say No.

Obviously, the best and surest way to avoid pregnancy was to avoid getting mostly-naked with a very special someone altogether—*Just Say No*. Practice it with me right now. *Just Say No*. Good for you. All you need to do now is to remember to *Just Say No* the very next time you meet someone who takes your fancy. This is significantly easier with someone you've just met online and are sharing a coffee-flavoured beverage with and have not recently married. It's much harder then.

Abstinence worked well, especially if a woman was married to someone she didn't actually want to have sex with. Perhaps she'd married or been married off as part of an alliance or to secure some really great real estate. In those cases, citing unwanted pregnancy seemed a legitimate escape.

How well did it work for someone who was married to a drop-dead gorgeous farm-boy with abs of steel? Only if a lady had a cast iron willpower one hundred percent of the time.

Edith and Geoffrey are a young couple with five small children. Mercifully, they are all tucked up in bed, sound asleep. The candle is burning low and Edith is looking particularly pretty tonight. A certain stirring is causing Geoffrey to be grateful it's a Tuesday, and he pulls his wife towards him...

Geoffrey: *Mmm... Edith... You look lovely tonight.*

Edith: *Thank you, my darling. As do you.*

Geoffrey: *I was thinking...well...it's been a whilst... Might we put that candle out and uh...you know?*

Edith: *Sleep? But I'm not tired.*

Geoffrey: *Me neither. I wasn't thinking sleep.*

Edith: *Oh! Um. Oh, umm. No.*

Geoffrey: *It's been such a long time...*

Edith: *But we have five babes already, and surely, we should have another if we do!*

Geoffrey: *Oh. No, then? Are you sure?*

Eyeing Geoffrey as he takes his shirt off.

Edith: *Sorry, my love. I'm sure. It's a no.*

Geoffrey: *Really sure?*

Eyeing Geoffrey as he removes his hose.

Edith: *Ye-e-e-s-s. I'm sort of sure...*

Geoffrey: *Really, really, really sure?*

Eyeing Geoffrey as he removes his breeches.

Edith: *Uh, well... I mean...*

Nine months later, baby number six is born.

Substitute Pussy

If a woman *is* able to *Just Say No*, she may decide to just pass on sex and men altogether and get a bunch of cats to side-track her and make her think less about forcing men to have sex with her. Surely, that would be a sensible and distracting option. Even nuns were allowed a cat for a companion since they were so useful and kept the rodent population down. Say no, get a cat. Cats were probably the answer.

If a woman was to become a cat owner, she would need to know what the best kind of cat to get might be. Imported kittens were the best kind. Albertus Magnus, born in 1200, wrote about cats in his treatise *De animalibus* and had this to say about them:

The animal loves to be lightly stroked by human hands and is playful, especially when young. When it sees its own image in a mirror it plays with that. It especially likes warm places and can be kept home more easily if its ears are

clipped since it cannot tolerate the night dew dripping into its ears. The wild ones are all grey in colour, but the domestic ones have various colours. They have whiskers around their mouth and if these are cut off they lose their boldness.

Adding another level of cuteness to the description of cats is Thomas de Cantimpré who was a Dominican friar and wrote extensively about nature in the thirteenth century. He sounds very much like a man who was a cat lover himself when he wrote:

They delight in being stroked by the hand of a person and they express their joy with their own form of singing.

I've not heard anything cuter.

Marginalia cat beating a cymbal. c. 1300.

Walters Art Museum, Baltimore. MS W.102 folio 78v

Isabella d'Este of Venice

We know many noble ladies kept cats for pets, some more exotic than others, and Isabella was one of these. She was born in 1474 and lived in Venice at the exact same time when Persian or Syrian cats were being imported and were what every woman wanted. They had tabby striped coats and were very rare. Over the course of many years, she had a couple of females imported for her at great expense, one with spots. At the age of thirty-one, she appears to have tired of relying on others to bring her kittens with acceptable level of cuteness and asked that she be brought a male and a female from Damascus.

Keeping cats, however, came with its own unique peril. Our Hildegard, whom we have come to know and love, isn't down on cats *per se*, though she feels that they are not perhaps the best companion if they've been licking things and are pregnant themselves. She advises:

> *The cat is not willingly with a person, except the one who feeds it. At the time when it licks toads and serpents, its heat is harmful and poisonous. When it carries its young within, its heat stirs up lust in a person; at other times it is not harmful for a person.*

Pregnant cats are lust-inducing? If this is true, then animal shelters must be a hotbed of repressed sexual energy. Who knew? Hopefully, the staff *Just Say No*.

Pulling Out

If a sweet young thing can't *Just Say No*, perhaps she could convince her partner to *Just Stop*! Coitus interruptus was definitely an option that required no external fixings and allowed a lovely lady to Say Yes.

That should work, right? No sperm, no baby. This was a practice recommended only a little bit for those who lacked the willpower to not have marital relations at all. And you can already guess which section of the community were just not that keen on recommending it.

Spilling the seed of the husband was also on the list of things condemned by the church at all stages, although the French theologian and archbishop Peter Paludanus, also known as Petrus de Palude, reluctantly agreed that coitus interruptus, that is, not completing the sex act before the release of the male seed, might be *less* sinful if employed by the husband to avoid having more children than he can feed. It was still a sin, just a slightly less terrible one.

We know that in some instances, this method was used.

There was a certain woman who went to court stating that she had been raped. To further her claim, she complained that the man responsible had also fouled her dress, which was quite probably a reference to her attacker withdrawing at the last moment in order to avoid pregnancy.

His seed spilled on her clothing and her not understanding what had happened had led to her complaint. Spilling seed was also a sin, but not quite as much as rape. Either way, the accused was not punished as there were no witnesses and it came down to a simple case of his word against hers.

Downers

If one couldn't be trusted to say no thanks or stop, the next best thing was to quench those flames of desire altogether before things got out of hand. Here, herbals might also once again be helpful. Hooray for herbs!

Although writing from antiquity, Aristotle had some recommendations on passion-killers which were still recommended and prescribed right into the middle of the medieval period. He suggested herbals like black and white henbane, melon, lead, lettuce seed, lily, coriander, chaste tree, rue, and camphor. A quick glance over the list reveals that along with passion, he was quite likely to kill the person taking it. He appeared unwilling to give directions for use, just mentioning that the herbals would take desire away. I'll bet.

More helpful and more willing to give instructions was our wonderful advisor Hildegard von Bingen. She had ideas on quenching lust in either the man or the woman or both. Being a nun, perhaps these might be of actual practical assistance?

Maybe. Don't try these at home.

To take away any desire from the man, she recommends:

> **Dill:** *In order for a man to extinguish the pleasure and lust of the flesh which is in him, he should, in Summer, take dill and twice as much water mint, and a little more tithymal, and the root of the Illyrian iris. He should put all these in vinegar, and make a condiment from them, and frequently eat it with all his foods.*

And by *he*, I'm thinking that the lady might like to make it and serve it. He'll never know.

What else? Java Pepper was an ingredient unlikely to be found in many Medieval kitchens, but Hildegard mentions it anyway.

> ***Java Pepper****: Java pepper is hot, but the heat has moderation in it. It is also dry. If anyone eats it, it tempers the shameful ardour which is in him. It brings joy to his mind and makes pure his thinking and disposition (as its beneficial, moderate heat extinguishes the unworthy passions of lust, in which fetid, slimy mucuses lie hidden, and clarifies a person's mind and his disposition by illuminating them).*

Indeed. Begone fetid mucus and foul thoughts! Sounds great! It may even work wonders of the mucuses in other body parts, like sinuses, who knows? Actually, there are other remedies for that. Pepper is hard to get hold of, anyway.

Perhaps you're a lady looking for something a little easier to get hold of in some areas? Look to lettuce. Wild lettuce is apparently good to quell those flames as well, but this remedy requires that he actually wants to quench them himself.

> **Wild lettuce:** *Wild lettuce is cold and it extinguishes lust in a human. A man who has an overabundance in his loins should cook wild lettuce in water and pour that water over himself in a sauna bath. He should also place the warm lettuce around his loins, whilst still in the sauna.*

An overabundance in his loins, you say? Something ought to be done about that quick smart. I must admit that cooked lettuce really doesn't sound terribly sexy. I'm also not sure that pouring it hot over a naked body in a sauna is the right way to go about less sex. Thank you anyway, Hildegard.

Don't throw out that lettuce just yet, ladies! You can use it for yourself, also. To take away a woman's own personal, uncontrollable lust as well as his, she recommends this:

> *If a woman's womb is swelling with uncontrollable lust, she should make a sauna bath of wild lettuce. Sitting in the sauna, she should pour the water in which the lettuce was cooked over the hot stones. She should place the warm, cooked lettuce over her belly. She should do this often. It will chase lust from her without diminishing the health of her body. Indeed, anyone with uncontrollable lust should dry wild lettuce in the sun and reduce it to a powder in his hand. They should often drink this powder in warm wine. It will extinguish the lust, with no damage to the body.*

More sauna and wine as well! I'm feeling a little doubtful about the extinguishing of the lust with this method. I really am.

Natural Contraception

Breastfeeding and poor nutrition provided a certain amount of contraceptive measure for a peasant woman, which was fortunate as these measures were free. Women in higher society were more likely to have wet nurses and better diets and thereby ran the risk of repeated pregnancy sooner than their poorer counterparts. Since pregnancy impeded a noble woman's lifestyle somewhat, there was a definite interest in contraceptive measures. Was there much for her to try?

Yes. There was.

She might like to jump up and down, post-coitus, to shake the seed out. It's not quite as romantic as snuggling in his arms on his chest in the rosy afterglow that many ladies prefer, but if energetic exercise might avoid a pregnancy, sure. Give it a shot. Leave the room if you think your partner might think you a little bit unhinged with your leaping and jumping. Bonus points if you can make this look natural and not in any way weird.

She might sneeze and hope for expulsion, which works a little bit, as any woman who has accidentally sneezed moments after a particularly frisky evening knows. I think I speak for most women here when I say the third best thing about condoms, apart from the nonpregnancy and the protection from sexually transmitted infections, is that it prevents this from ever happening. If one finds that spontaneous sneezing is impossible, perhaps keep a little pepper shaker by the bed for those unplanned sexy emergencies. Actually, pepper was very expensive in the Middle Ages, so that's a hopeless idea.

She might also try to urinate immediately after coitus and hope the seed would be washed away. I can see the thought process behind that one, and a good rinse sounds like a sensible idea, providing one can summon a stream of urine exactly when needed. According to Magnus, that last one was a viable option.

Chastity Belts

Surely, if Hollywood has taught us anything, it's that chastity belts were a thing and they were to avoid rape and pregnancy and that Medieval women wore them *all the time* in Ye Olde Medieval Days of Yore. Yes?

Uh, no.

Stories of women being locked into their belts whilst their menfolk rode heroically off to crusade for years on end and took the keys with them, or left them with a trusted friend, sounds

like it just might be something that happened, but it falls down on a number of key elements.

Chastity belts aren't mentioned at the time of the actual crusades.

They aren't mentioned in inventories and aren't written about in medical journals which are dealing with any number of intimate complaints. They aren't alluded to in literature. Sex toys are written, okay, complained about, but not chastity belts. There's the first problem.

The existing ones date far after the time they were supposedly first worn. In the main medieval period, from 1300 to 1500, we find no written instructions for women who are travelling to wear one to protect their virtue whilst they are on the road. This would be the time they would be most helpful and when a woman was more likely to encounter a rape or abduction situation. There's nothing. We have written instructions for everything from making glue from cheese and not looking too far ahead when a person walks in the town, to how to make ink from axel grease, but no instructions on wearing any kind of personal protection for her own safety or his own ease of mind. Not a word.

The idea seems to have come from a later time period—Victorians, I'm looking at you—looking backwards and writing stories. As for contemporary evidence? I see none. James Cleugh, in his book *Love Locked Out*, states that chastity belts were becoming common in the twelfth century and that duplicate keys were easy to make, but on what gave him that idea, he is mystifyingly silent.

Belting Up

The first crusades took place in the Holy Lands well before when the first actual chastity belt makes it first appearance. All information we have today suggests that even though the first one probably appeared around the sixteenth or, more likely, seventeenth century, they were, in fact, uncommon.

When one was found in Linz, Austria by a German named Anton Pachinger, it caused great excitement and generated much discussion. An iron and leather belt was found on the skeleton of a young woman. The burial was dated to the sixteenth century, but no documentation could be found of her burial in the town's records, which made the burial date a bit questionable. The belt itself had been lost to history when Anton died, preventing further analysis of the item in question.

Further chastity belts have been exhibited by the Musée de Cluny in France.

Catherine de Medici of Italy

The first of two was attributed to Catherine de Medici and is best described as a simple velvet-covered hoop and plate of iron. Catherine was a noblewoman who became the queen of France in the sixteenth century. She was educated by nuns in Florence and her uncle was the Pope Clement VIII. She was described as courteous, gay, energetic, and discrete, none of which seem to describe the kind of woman who would agree to be locked into a chastity belt for extended periods of time by a husband who was forcing her against her will.

Anne of Austria

The second of the pair is reputed to belong to Anne of Austria who was a Spanish princess and also a queen of France. She reigned in the seventeenth century. Anne was deeply religious, and she raised her younger siblings following the death of her mother who died giving birth. The chastity belt attributed to her is described as...

> *...a hinged pair of plates held about the waist by metal straps, featuring intricately etched figures of Adam and Eve.*

Whilst it sounds delightful, again, it is hard to imagine this woman willingly wearing such a device unless it was for her own protection against foul play whilst travelling. And the seventeenth century isn't what we consider today to be Medieval. The medieval period is usually considered to be from 1066 to 1485. The belt of Anne, if it *is* hers, is from two hundred years later.

This theory also falls apart by its conspicuous absence in other records. Why aren't chastity belts mentioned as a thing any lady travelling used is interesting. If they *were* worn for that reason, surely many books and stories would have mentioned it, and would there not be a roaring trade in these devices from every woman of good breeding who travelled and wanted a pair of safety protector pants? Sex toys get a mention, so why be shy about this?

It doesn't add up.

As well as those two most notable ones attached to two royal ladies who probably didn't wear them, not having name tags sewn into them and all, were there others we might examine? Yes and no. The British Museum and the Germanisches Nationalmuseum both had some on display which have now been removed. On the whole, modern historians are dating them more at the nineteenth century rather than the medieval period. It's also interesting to note that there are as many existing male chastity belts as there are female ones, each designed to stop arousal with spikes pointing inwards around the groin. Those crazy Victorians.

So, as a contraceptive device, it falls quite short. Not being invented yet, and all.

Condoms

What about condoms? A cover made to cover the entire of the male member seems like it was a thing known of for an indefinite amount of time. Condoms were used in ancient Roman times, so seems like a reasonable suggestion. For no real practical reason other than religion taking a bit of a moral stand about seed being wasted, condoms appear to fade from the archaeological record after the Romans withdrew, only to surprisingly reappear in fifteenth century.

The oldest excavated extant condoms which were made from animal product, a thin skin designed to be worn over the penis, was discovered in a cesspit at Dudley Castle. The multiple condoms dated back to 1642, and it is theorised that they were worn by soldiers in the king's court at that time. Those condoms were reusable and made from animal intestines. And they possibly weren't used for contraception, but for prevention of disease.

As far as condoms to prevent pregnancy go, they are more Renaissance than Medieval. Nothing earlier than that then? Actually, yes. In the sixteenth century, the Italians were making discoveries of their own.

The Italian Sheaths

In 1564 Italy, Gabriele Falloppio wrote about *The French Disease*, most likely referring to syphilis. He recommended a new invention of his own—linen sheaths soaked in a chemical solution and allowed to dry before use.

They covered only the glans of the penis and were held on with a ribbon, which sounds quite festive. Italian fashion was quite festooned with ribbons and laces at that time, so it really comes as no great surprise. Again, these were not used for birth control, but purely to avoid catching something unpleasant. Covering only the tip doesn't seem to be a sure-fire way of avoiding a sexually transmitted disease, but the certain solution it was soaked in may have had some merit. We don't know what it was because he seemed quite reluctant to share his trade secret.

As with any good invention, a degree of testing might have been needed in the name of science to make sure it actually

worked. The inventive Fallopio claimed to have performed an experimental trial, in what was essentially a clinical trial. His linen sheath was tested, according to him, on one thousand one hundred men and he reported that none of them had contracted the dreaded disease. One hundred percent success rate.

Either the solution he soaked the sheaths in was exceptionally powerful, or the men who took part in the trial were reluctant to be honest about catching things. Can you imagine getting volunteers for that? Men! Sign up for some guaranteed free sexy times which you may or may not be sorry for...ladies also needed...uh...nice girls need not apply.

Fallopio has been super busy for the past week making his little glans protectors and sewing ribbons onto them. They looked simply smashing, and all he needs now were willing participants to test them out.

Fallopio: *Hurry! Hurry! Free sex if you volunteer to try my new product!*

Crowd starts to gather.

Fallopio: *Try out my new sheaths! Free sheaths! All you need to do is put these on thy privy member and fornicate with some lovely ladies! It's free! And you get to have sex! For free!*

Man 1: *Free? Really? What do I have to do?*

Man 2: *I'm interested in free sex.*

Fallopio: *For free! All the sex you want as long as you wear one of my new inventions!*

Man 2: *Your new what? What's it do?*

Fallopio: *Well, it's...you put it on your privy member before the free sex!*

Man 1: *I'll have some free sex!*

Man 2: *Uh, what's the invention do? The...what was it... sheath?*

Fallopio: *All-natural linen! Hand spun! Sustainably grown! And it's free!*

Man 1: *I am so ready for this!*

Man 2: *But the sheath?*

Fallopio: *Oh, it's just to stop you catching syphilis from one of the women. And it's free!*

Man 1: *Wait, what?*

Man 2: *Wait, what?*

Crickets chirping.

Fallopio: *I also need a bunch of skanky women.*

So, there were condoms for infectious disease prevention of sorts, but no condoms for birth control.

What then, might a Medieval woman do to take steps to be actively Not Pregnant?

Prescribed Contraceptives

Rather surprisingly, some Medieval women did know about, and use, contraception. Since childbirth was so perilous, many women wanted to not have babies—a lifestyle choice that was clearly condemned by the church. St Augustine declared that any woman, whether she was married or otherwise, became a whore in the eyes of God if she used contraceptives, as the only reason for sexual intercourse was procreation.

St. Bernadino made no effort to hide his feelings either. He wrote strongly against husbands who practised sex positions and acts which fell into the *against nature* category, but he was abundantly clear that far worse than that was any women who practised contraception. His scathing words equated them with murderers.

And I say this to the women who are the cause that the children that they have conceived are destroyed; worse,

> *who also are amongst those who arrange that they cannot conceive; and if they have conceived, they destroy them in the body. You are more evil than murderers.*

Two thirteenth-century treatises, Magnus's *De Secretis Mulierum* from sometime between 1206 and 1280 CE, and John XXI's *The Treasury of Healthe* from 1276, offer a variety of contraceptive methods that might be employed. The *Treasury of Healthe* alone included twenty-six different prescriptions to try.

Debates on contraception for a woman who had previous complications with pregnancy were held with great seriousness at the highest level of the church. Should a woman refrain from sex so that she might not conceive and possibly die in childbirth when sex was so necessary for her health and well-being? Were contraceptives permissible in situations such as these? Weighty matters were debated vigorously.

St Augustine Book of Hours Cambria dated between 1450 and 1460. Walters Ex Libris. W240_ folio 330v.

Delicate or Young Women

One medical text written by William of Saliceto, *Summa Conservationis et Curationis*, echoed the *Canon of Medicine* by Avicenna. William had strong feelings about contraception, but also wrote with a bit more kindness about preventing conception in certain cases:

> *...although this chapter may not be according to the strict rules of law (demandato legis), nevertheless, for*

the ordinary course of medical science on account of the danger that comes to a woman because of a dangerous risk of conceiving on account of her health, debilities, or the extremity of her youth.

Consideration for a woman who was unwell or of a delicate constitution was a good idea which William reluctantly acknowledged.

The *extremity of her youth* is a concerning phrase, hinting that a girl may be physically able to fall pregnant, but be seen as too young to successfully sustain a pregnancy or birth a child. It also hints that the situations which occur for a pregnancy to happen certainly were happening. If she wasn't at risk, the need to prevent a pregnancy would no longer be there.

Knowing that a girl might be married very young if she was an heiress and might be able to fall pregnant as young as nine years old—this is point blank alarming. In situations like these, might it not be better to avoid impregnating the child by waiting until she's older? No?

That's a shame.

God's will in all matters stretched far into the marital bed. If God wanted a woman to have babies, and she was taking steps to not have babies, this was a serious offence. It might not be proven that a wife was taking contraception to prevent further pregnancies, but it might be suspected.

Choosing to thwart the baby-making plans God had for a person might have dire consequences, as they did for the Countess of Flanders, Clementia, in the twelfth century.

Clementia of Flanders

Robert II and his wife Clementia married, and within the next three years, she bore him three fine, strapping sons. After this, she failed to conceive again. A very questioning monk, Henmann

de Tournai, suspiciously accused Clementia of using *feminine arts* to prevent further pregnancies.

Apparently, she feared the children she already had would not have any inheritance left if she continued to fall pregnant and produce children year after year. How he knew that, we don't know, but since she was a good church-going woman, there was every chance that he had heard her say as much to him herself from the confessional.

Henmann, who comes across as being particularly uncompassionate for a man of the cloth, was unsurprised when God punished Clementia by causing all three of her boys to die whilst young. As far as he was concerned, she had been punished for daring to assume that she knew better than her creator about what was good for her. God had spoken, and Henmann was on his side.

Whether Clementia had been taking some kind of preventative measures or not, she disappears from the records and fails to have further children. From a medical point of view, this would indicate more that she may have had problems with her last pregnancy which had made her unable to fall pregnant again. If she had been taking a contraceptive, she would more likely have continued to have further pregnancies to replace the three sons she had lost.

We really don't know for sure.

Charms

Getting back to contraception. What else might the Medieval woman try?

Remedies start with herbals and charms. Whilst charms were nothing more than a placebo guaranteed not to work, herbals could offer some help. In a study of one thirteenth-century French village, Montaillou, we learn of a woman who is given an herbal charm to wear so she would not conceive.

Beatrice de Plainisolles of Montaillou

The widow Beatrice was about to enter into an illicit relationship with Pierre Clergue, her priest, and had some initial misgivings. She asked what she should do, for if she became pregnant by him, she should be lost and ashamed. Pierre wasn't one to take no for an answer so easily. They would take precautions.

> *I have a certain herb. If a man wears it when he mingles his body with that of a woman, he cannot engender, nor she conceive.*

Beatrice seemed a bit sceptical, and who can blame her? She wanted to know the exact nature of the herb and had many questions.

> *What sort of herb? Is it the one the cowherds hang over a cauldron of milk in which they have put some rennet, to stop the milk from curdling as long as the herb is over the cauldron?*

Whilst using the rennet of a hare in other contraceptive recipes seemed rather astute, it was also a bit perplexing. Why would an anti-curdling herb help prevent conception? Easy. The herb prevented the milk from curdling into cheese and would therefore produce the same effect on male semen, stopping it from solidifying into a foetus.

An illicit union resulting in a child.

Hague KB 71A. 24 folio 15.

With logic such as that, Pierre convinced Beatrice that all would be well, and since she was not so much

concerned with the sin of fornicating with a man of the cloth but of pregnancy related to him, she consented. She tells her story:

> *When Pierre Clergue wanted to know me carnally, he used to wear this herb wrapped up in a piece of linen, about an ounce long and wide, or about the size of the first joint of my little finger. And he had a long cord which he used to put round my neck whilst we made love; and this thing or herb at the end of the cord used to hang down between my breasts, as far as the opening of my stomach. When the priest wanted to get up and leave the bed, I would take the thing and give it back to him. It might happen that he wanted to know me carnally twice or more in a single night; in that case the priest would ask me, before uniting his body with mine, "where is the herb?"*

Pierre was a priest, so it was vital that his lovers not become with child by him. Whilst it was okay for him to be messing around with any number of available, single women, it wasn't okay for them to be also messing around with others.

Pierre went as far as to remove the charm and take it with him whilst he was away from Beatrice to ensure her fidelity. He refused to leave it with her, even when she asked him to, on the grounds that she might use the herb to fornicate with someone else. Especially his cousin Pathau who was her ex-lover.

Pierre assured her that any shame she might feel at being pregnant and a widow reflected on her father only whilst he was alive, and that once he had died, he would like to make Beatrice pregnant.

Hopefully, Beatrice came to her senses well before then.

One feels that the benefits of any given herbs might be the most helpful when consumed rather than worn on a necklace. But I'm not a doctor, so I can't be sure.

The Abbess and the Charm

In a similar story found in the *Facetiae* written by Poggio Bracciolini, a monk and an abbess have an illicit sexual liaison. As with Beatrice, the abbess is afraid of becoming pregnant. The persuasive monk gives to her a necklace to wear whilst they make love which will surely prevent a child resulting from their sexual congress. The necklace is nothing more than a folded piece of paper with what he tells her is a charm. Not surprisingly, very soon afterwards, the abbess becomes pregnant and the monk leaves her.

Bewildered at how the charm has failed, she unfolds the piece of paper to read what is written and is aghast to see:

> *"Asca imbarasca, non facias te supponi, et non implebis tascam."*

Translated, it said—"Don't let yourself get laid, and you will not fill the cup." Truer words were never spoken.

Other preventative remedies ranged from the mildly unlikely to work to the outright bizarre, although they were used with all seriousness. I've chosen my four favourites with a sliding scale of possible success.

Contraceptive Blocks

On the "most likely to work" list and the most sensible contraceptive measure recorded is the barrier method, which came from Germany. Women there, apparently, had ingeniously used beeswax and rags to form a physical block like a tampon. This is actually quite a good solution. The rags roll up and block the opening to the uterus and the wax would make a reasonably good barrier.

The most obvious contraceptive block would appear to be a contraceptive sponge, so how about those? Did Medieval women

use sponges? The historical records we have are sketchy. We see them here and there, but not during the Middle Ages. Why not? It's a mystery. As a method of soaking up sperm to prevent conception, it's certainly better than nothing and might be washed and reused.

No record comes to us from the usual sources of things women shouldn't do: the church. No sermons, no confession articles. Nothing.

Douches

On the "quite likely to work but will also kill you list"—douching with or eating lead.

Seriously, don't eat lead. Or rinse out your most private parts with it. It will kill you. Calling one's partner a douche in the medieval period may also result in a swift lack of sex, which, in turn, leads to a lack of baby making. Or earns you a severe and brutal beating. Either way, not terribly likely to lead to sex.

Animal Concoctions

On the "I bet that works but not for the reason you think" list, we again hear from the famed lady medic from the early medieval period, Trotula, who was always helpful with a remedy or two for the woman with issues. She offers this wonderful advice:

> *Take a male weasel and let its testicles be removed and let it be released alive. Let the woman carry these testicles with her in her bosom and let her tie them in goose skin or in another skin, and she will not conceive.*

Call me sceptical, but do I actually think that this would work? I don't. I feel that weasel testicles wrapped in goose skin dangling between the breasts is more than likely to make sure your husband doesn't come near enough to you to try anything likely to result in pregnancy.

Test it tonight when you get home, if you like, and see how it goes.

Actually, don't. Aside from the whole I-don't-think-it will-actually-keep-you-from-impending-motherhood, I feel that getting your hands on a couple of quality medical-grade weasel testicles may be a problem. If you're the kind of person who is not that easily deterred, I'd like to remind you that the weasel must be released alive post-testicle removal.

Instructions must be followed to the letter if these things are expected to work.

John and Alice are finishing off dinner. It's been a good day and Alice had checked the calendar in the hope that there might be a little romantic involvement this evening. It's a Tuesday, and there is no feast day to observe. She has her coif on and all that remains is to lure her husband to the bedroom.

Alice: *Oh, Joooohnnnnn.*

John: *I like the sound of that!*

Alice: *It's Tuesday.*

John: *All right!*

Alice: *There's no feast day today.*

John: *All riiight!*

Alice: *And I'm wearing my coif!*

John: *Ohmygod, all riiiight! I love the sound of that!*

Alice: *So just come a little closer and I'll blow this candle out...*

John: *Uh, Alice. Wait. What's that?*

Alice: *Oh, that's my protection. So I won't get pregnant. Come closer, my darling...*

John: *It kinda smells; what's in it?*

Alice: *Nothing special, just some goose skin. Come closer...*

John: *It's really rancid. Take it off.*

Alice. *Oh, I can't do that. Besides, it's probably just the weasel testicles. Come to me...*

John: *Did you just say weasel testicles? You have weasel testicles?*

Alice: *It's nothing, My love...come closer. Let me fulfil your desires...*

John: *I desire you to take that fetid stink off from around your neck.*

Alice: *I'm not taking it off! I don't want to get pregnant tonight. I'm not taking it off.*

John: *If you're not taking it off, I don't think you'll be getting pregnant. Rolls over. Goodnight.*

Voilà! Not pregnant!

Now, contraception wasn't just for the lady. Oh no. You'll be delighted to hear that Medieval medicine was quite forward-thinking, and also included contraception for men. This was great news for the sexually active lady who devoutly wished to be Not Pregnant. If she could talk her husband into it. Let's see how likely that might be, shall we?

Male Contraceptives

Rather excitingly, men were also able to do their bit to avoid making babies, using nothing more than things they might have in the garden. We have very few records for male contraceptives, but they are really fantastic ones.

You'll need your gardening gloves for this one. A plaster made of hemlock, yes, hemlock (now there's a harmless plant for you) applied to the testicles of the husband prior to the sex act was also recommended. Hemlock, gosh.

In a roundabout way, this may have had long-term success. One imagines that repeated applications of one of the world's deadliest plants to one of man's most sensitive places possibly did not bode terribly well for the general health of the man. However, do remember, a dead man can't impregnate anyone, so it succeeds quite well in that respect. Just a reminder, don't try it at home, even if you do have some hemlock lying around the kitchen and are feeling romantic. Just don't.

Surprisingly, or not, this helpful advice comes from a treatise written by the future Catholic Pope John XXI in *The Treasure of the Poor*. It's a little telling on both his grasp of dangerous herbs and his feelings towards poor people, really. The challenge for the lady might be talking her unwilling husband into smearing a paste of anything on his genitals, let alone poison. Just how the future Pope figured that one out or who advised him that this was a really, really good idea, we are not informed.

Even earlier than this, the writings of Aristotle thoughtfully recommended rubbing cedar oil onto the penis. How this was supposed to be beneficial, I am also uncertain. To the medically untrained layperson, *rubbing* and *penis* often equate much less with lack of pregnancy and much more towards enflaming passions and situations likely to lead down the path of deep regrets. I'm told.

Abortion

For those who didn't practice contraception, or for those who did with poor results, another option was to terminate the unwanted child or bring on the menses when they were late. Or *late* late, if you follow my meaning.

The deliberate act of terminating an unborn foetus was viewed quite harshly by ecclesiastic counts. Usually, it was equated with murder.

In both civil and canon law in thirteenth-century England, abortion was condoned in certain conditions only—in the case of an unborn child endangering the life of the mother, it was the life of the mother that was to be saved. Nevertheless, quite a lot was written about the certain herbs and practices for ending an unwanted pregnancy. It was known to be quite dangerous and, as you can imagine, was clearly severely frowned upon by pretty much everyone.

It would be naïve of us to pretend that pregnancies were never brought to an end before their time, so we shall look at some of the methods that were used. These methods were usually described for the bringing forth a dead child from the womb, not a living one, but the methods would work just as well for either, not that they seem particularly good at all. Modern scholars have written extensively on whether or not the existence of these prove they were used for terminations in the case of unwanted babies, but the truth is, we don't know.

Herbal Compounds

Whilst herbs were not terribly reliable as a contraceptive, they were to be handled with great care when used to expel a foetus. We know of popular herbal compounds using rosemary and balsam with or without parsley and consuming myrrh and coriander to bring about a late period. Late period. Hmm.

Again, the question of whether the period is late or a pregnancy is suspected is a factor here. Amongst the herbs we know, wormwood is a notoriously bitter herb reputed to induce miscarriage.

English law gave some clearly defined rules about this:

He who oppresses a pregnant woman, or gives to her a poison, or delivers to her a blow so as to cause an abortion, or who gives to her (something) that she will not conceive, if the foetus is formed and animated, is guilty of homicide.

It is mentioned that the unborn child must be animated, that is, moving in the mother's womb. And if that wasn't clear enough, it repeats itself, with particular reference to the fact that the unborn baby is moving:

A woman commits homicide who so devastates an animated child through a drink or similar things in the stomach.

In spite of this, women came before the civil and religious courts faced with crimes of aborting a child by means of herbal preparations.

Joan Willys of Harpenden

In the records of the Visitations of the diocese of Lincoln, England from 1530, we find one John Hunt, who had gotten his servant with child and took dire actions to avoid impending parenthood.

Harpenden. John Hunt lives incontinently with Joan Willys, his servant... Afterwards they appeared at the Priory od St Giles and confessed that they had contracted marriage together. Also that we charge you that you gave the said woman advice and persuaded her to take and to drink certain drinks to destroy the child that she is with.

Unfortunately for John, he was forced to marry Joan quick smart the very next day. How Joan felt about marrying the man who forced her to lose her baby is not recorded.

It seems to be the same story we see so often. The man takes advantage of his servant girl, gets her into bed by promising her

marriage, gets her pregnant, persuades her to take measures to be Not Pregnant, and then marries her when he has absolutely no other choice.

The Herbalist's Customer of Somerset

A number of the cases do make it to court, but rarely spare a thought for the young woman who gets no justice at all and is left to fend for herself, with or without a child. It's quite rare that the finger of blame is pointed towards the people supplying the herbs and compounds for this, but we have one slightly amusing written reference from a very angry herbalist from Somerset, England.

He not only went to court, but very publicly named and shamed an unmarried woman who had used the herbal compound he supplied to successfully rid herself on an unwanted child. He states quite vehemently:

> *...the whore should have paid for them.*

It's a little harsh, considering she got the means from him. His angst stemmed entirely not from the fact that the woman was behaving in an unchaste manner, but because she didn't pay him for them. What a strumpette.

Medical treatises had advice, as usual, on remedies for this particular ailment. Hildegard von Bingen wasn't too keen to give advice on herbs to specifically abort a foetus, but she warns that some herbs will affect a pregnant woman that way and that care must be taken:

> ***Goatsbeard.*** *Goatsbeard is cold and harsh. Goatsbeard's nature is thus that it is always accustomed to break whatever exists in the place it resides. So it dashes to pieces whatever is fetid, where it finds it. Also, if a pregnant woman eats it, it causes her to abort, with great danger to her body.*

In this instance, she is not recommending the herb, but warning against the use of it.

The Demon-Raped Woman of Lincoln

Hugh of Lincoln, who was a bishop in the very last years of the twelfth century, carefully considered his remedies to fit their symptoms. When one of his parishioners was raped by a demon in the form of a young man and came to him for help, Hugh advocated the use of St John's wort to ensure that no pregnancy might occur.

His theory was quite sound. St John's wort was used to treat snake bites, and to his thinking, there was no reason why it wasn't the ideal product to combat the *venom* of the ancient serpent or demon who had raped her. This, he felt, was because anything that might provide malice in the world would have a remedy provided by God. Even the *bite* of a young-man-shaped demon.

Fumigation and Pessaries

Trotula, always to be counted on in time of a medical crisis, suggested that iris root inserted into the womb or fumigated from below would make a mother lose her child, but was only to be used if the pregnancy was sure to cause loss of life to the mother. In this special circumstance, a baptised adult took precedence over an unbaptised child.

> *Also the root of iris put into the womb or fumigated underneath makes a woman lose her child, for iris roots are hot and dry and have the virtue of opening, heating, consuming, and wasting. For when woman is feeble and the child cannot come out, then it is better that the child be killed than the mother of the child also die.*

In another version of the Trotula, instructions to bring on a purgation of the menses instructs:

> *The matter may be brought down with sweet-smelling things, take the oil of musk and do thus: take two and a half gallons of good, suitable oil that is very sweet and add to it one pound of pennyroyal, half a pound each of rosemary, costmary, camomile, lavender, balm, woodruff, hyssop, savory, shaving of cypress, twelve drachms of calamint, feverfew, fennel, wormwood, sage, rue, orginanum, southernwood, mugwort of St Johns. Wash them first in water, then boil in malmsey, grind them up, put them in the previously mentioned oil, add to the mixture a quart of wine. Let them boil right down, pass them through a good, new, wide-meshed canvas to clean them. For this oil is good for all kinds of sickness that occur, especially for cold and for the suffocation of the womb.*

Bringing on the menses might be nothing more than bringing about a late period, but as it was known to make this happen, it could also have been used in the very earliest days of pregnancy when contraception had not been used and it was possible pregnancy had occurred. All the parties concerned needed to pretend this was not the case in order to avoid the frowny face of the clerics and the judgement of family and friends.

Breaking the Womb

If a woman didn't wish to fumigate from below, insert something within, or take an herbal potion, she knew that excessive strenuous exercise might cause her to lose her baby.

Obviously, her daily chores were not to be ignored, and her daily grind would continue as usual, especially if she was a woman in the country with chickens to feed, cows to milk, gardens to tend, and domestic chores to tend to. Washing and cooking wasn't

going to do itself, and even if she had a servant to assist her, she would be expected to shoulder her usual workload. Unnecessarily hard work or extremely strenuous activity might cause a miscarriage, however.

Magnus warned of this in his *On the Exit of the Fetus from the Uterus* and hinted that certain women may work with the express purpose of breaking the womb and ending a pregnancy.

> *...either because the matter of the menses is corrupt, or because of too much motion on the part of the woman which breaks the womb, or on account of other evils that befall her. For this reason, harlots, and women learned in the art of midwifery, engage in a good deal of activity when they are pregnant. They move from place to place, town to town: they lead dances and take part in many other evil deeds. Even more frequently they have a great deal of sex, and they wrestle with men. They do all these things so that they might be freed from their pregnancy by the excessive motion.*

If this method of terminating a pregnancy was used, a woman could certainly state that she was doing no more than her usual work and that this was nothing more than the will of God that she should lose her unborn baby.

Accidents happen, after all.

The Gilbertine Nun of Yorkshire

After all is said and done, if pregnancy occurs and it shouldn't have, a woman might pray. God would sort her out. This was exactly the approach taken by a nun who had been a little careless with her chastity in 1166.

Her choice of partner did nothing to recommend her; he was a lay brother. This unnamed nun lived in Yorkshire at Watton. Unfortunately for the woman, she became pregnant, but, as the

story goes, God took pity on her and *annulled* the pregnancy. Abbot Alired of Rievaulx's words, not mine.

This mercy didn't sit entirely well with the rest of the nuns who decided that vengeance wasn't to be left to God and it wasn't above them to give Him a helping hand. The nun's sisters ambushed her and her lover, forced her to castrate him and...

> *...had thrust the parts into her mouth.*

Marginalia Nun. Initial "A" with the Resurrection and three Marys at the tomb.

Beaupré Antiphonary, Volume 1, Walters Ex Libris. W. 759. Folio H18.

Speechless, in more ways than one, describes the situation here. The amount of peer group pressure involved to talk a person into cutting off their own lover's bits is staggering.

Why didn't she just refuse? Exactly what did they say to her? Did they have more than one knife? Once they gave her the knife to cut him with, why didn't she refuse then? Or cut one of them? That's the makings of a savage horror movie, right there.

Chapter 9

Forbidden Love

The amazing thing about the Middle Ages is that many of the concepts found in it were shockingly okay and not okay at the same time, depending on the circumstances. Forbidden love affairs fall into this category, and it is here that courtly love was revered and touted as the most romantic of all loves, whilst at the exact same time, the adultery it often resulted in was agreed to be completely sinful.

Courtly Love

The pile of books written on the subject of courtly love in the Middle Ages is immense. It is fair to say that a *substantial* amount has been penned describing it. With this in mind, we shall take a brief glimpse at the world of courtly love, what it was and how it came about, without diving too deeply into it.

Courtly love was the notion of a man, usually upper class and from the courtly circles, admiring, desiring, and actively courting a woman of unquestionable morals, who may or may not be another man's wife. She, of course, is unattainable, and his heart aches for the merest glance and sigh from her. He cannot sleep, and his heart should only be quieted by a kiss or gesture that she pines for him, also.

Her unavailability in no way stops him from giving her gifts, writing her songs, and composing her poetry. He yearns for her. The pain of not being able to consummate this heartfelt longing is absolute torture to him. He is incredibly angsty about the whole situation, whilst she steadfastly fails to let herself be wooed by his efforts. Interestingly enough, courtly love wasn't actually called courtly love at the time; that was a name applied retrospectively.

Silver-gilt fleur-de-lys brooch with decorated body from fourteenth-century France.

Artifact from the Gilbert Collection.

Tokens of Love

Andreas Capellanus, a twelfth-century author of De amore gives an insight into what dress accessories were available and could be given as a gift of love—

> *A lover may freely accept from her beloved these things—a handkerchief, a hairband, a circlet of gold or silver, a brooch for the breast, a mirror, a belt, a purse, a lace for clothes, a comb, cuffs, gloves, a ring, a little box of scent, a portrait, toiletries, little vases, trays, a standard as a keepsake of the lover, and so to speak more generally, a woman may accept from her love whatever gift may be useful in the care of her person, or may look charming, or may remind her of her lover, providing, however, that in accepting the gift it is clear that she is acting quite without avarice.*

It seemed perfectly harmless to give and receive little gifts and tokens of affection like those mentioned, but the proviso was that they not be given secretly. Secret gift-giving might be seen as clandestine. Public displays of a generous and loving heart were to be admired and accompanied with flowery speeches and aching hearts. Accepting something as precious as a circlet of gold might need to be handled carefully as the sheer expense of it was not a gift given lightly. Rings, also, were seen to be an appropriate gift, which today we might see as far too intimate to accept from a male admirer if one is married to someone else.

Troubadours

The word *troubadour* comes from the northern French word *trouveur*, or finder. The poet was thus called if he no longer repeated known popular stories, but instead, found new verses which were unheard.

In the eleventh century, the troubadours in Southern France and Aquitaine seemed to kick off the entire movement by expanding their usual repertoire of songs about manly deeds and heroic battles by introducing their new unrequited love theme. It was all very well doing many and heroic deeds, but to what purpose? What purpose? To impress the ladies! What they needed to do was convince everyone that the ladies were not mere chattels in a marriage, but were creatures well worth impressing.

A troubadour did this. Not only did he find the words required, but also found the lucky lady which he claimed he most certainly could not live or breathe without. There would be no sleep, no merriment in his heart, no smile on his lips, nor poem to recite without signs and favours from the object of his affection. Just a sign was enough. The slightest bit of encouragement would be all that was needed to suddenly provide inspiration for stanza after stanza of descriptive beauty and virtues possessed by a lady who may not have actually had them. Once one started it, the craze spread like wildfire.

It certainly didn't hurt that many of the patrons of the musicians were, in fact, the ladies themselves. Any sensible musician, when asked to describe the woman who is essentially paying his bills

and funding his lifestyle, is quite likely to say nice things about her. The whiteness of her skin, her noble brow and her beautiful lips. Her overall beauty. Her kindness and gentleness of heart. A woman who was a patron of the arts, was a woman well worth singing about. Men, naturally, looked at women in a fresh, new way. Suddenly, these wives and maidens were elevated into creatures of beauty and desire.

Matilda of Aquitaine

Matilda was born in 1156, the daughter of the rather famous Eleanor of Aquitaine, but she was also the Duchess of Saxony in her own right. Clearly, she was a woman who inspired men to compose courtly words about her, none more so than those of the lovelorn Bertram de Born, the Lord of Hauteford, who wistfully wrote:

> *The more one disrobes her, the more grows inclination and desire. Her dazzling bosom turns night into day. When the eye looks lower the whole words seems alight. How good it is to hold that blooming and supple form naked in one's arms!*

I'm not sure what quantifies a bosom as being dazzling enough to turn night into day, and I'm sure she would have liked him to keep the bit about her being supple to himself. It is a far cry from being Satan's bait, though.

Eleanor of Aquitaine

Not to be outdone, Eleanor had admirers of her own who waxed lyrical about her features. Eleanor was born in 1122 or 1124 in Poitiers, France, though details are a bit sketchy. Her life is told and retold in countless books, and indeed, it takes a book to tell her story alone, so here we shall just focus on the words she inspired. There is little doubt that she was actually beautiful and even when young, was called more than beautiful. The troubadour we know best penned these words about her:

> *I think I shall die unless my fair one invites me thither where she is wont to repose, that I may kiss and caress and strain in my arms her white, plump, smooth body.*

Which quite frankly seems to denote a level of familiarity beyond the most wistful acquaintanceship that most troubadours hoped for. These examples of sighing and wanting and wishing and yearning were very typical of the new rise which women of gentle birth were enjoying away from loathing. Certainly, women were not to be trusted because of their cold natures, but they might be admired and sighed over, too.

Romance tales became exceptionally popular during the fourteenth century. Stories of *Lancelot* by the writer Chretien de Troyes, who desperately yearned for King Arthur's wife Guinevere is the classic tale of courtly love, right up to the point where she finally caves in, consummates their relationship, and begins a secret, adulterous affair. We all know how it ends. Badly for everyone. Arthur loses his right-hand man and wife, Lancelot loses his king and his lover, and Guinevere joins a nunnery, takes the veil, and loses them both.

Romancing the Rose

The *Roman de la Rose*, or *Romance of the Rose* tells a lengthy tale of a wistful young lover who tries to win his lady's love and prove his worthiness at the same time whilst being sad about it a lot. It was written by Guillaume de Lorris from 1225 to 1230, but remained unfinished until completed by another writer, Jean de Meun, between 1269 and 1278. In his own words, Guillaume describes his story:

> *If any man or woman should ask what I wish this romance...to be called, it is the Romance of the Rose, in which the whole art of love is contained.*

There are a few beautifully illuminated manuscripts which show the hapless lover attempting to overcome obstacles to get to the object of his affection. He first needs to get past a number of virtues and vices personified who either attempt to help or hinder him. Why this hasn't been remade as an immersive role-playing online game with levels and bosses is a mystery to me. No cash or extra lives or bonuses, just love. (Once the big boss at the end is defeated.) The big boss who needs to be won over in this case is a Virtue called Fair Welcome, the writer having already defeated Reason, Jealousy, Wealth, and a host of others.

The final scene has our hero describing an amazing array of euphemisms for deflowering a virgin. The Lover reaches the tower, but the gate is closed and needs him to push his key in the lock. The entry is too narrow. Images sometimes show twin towers with a very narrow door between them which suggest the legs of a lady and her opening between. Early on in the story, we see that Nature had given the Lover a staff which he polished in the hope of using it shortly. You just can't beat subtlety like that, and the songs and stories of courtly love are just packed full of them.

Woman at the Tower.
Initial, Book of Hours, Walters Ex Libris. Manuscript W.277, Folio 75r.

Meanwhile, in Germany, the *minnesingers*, musician-poets of the twelfth century, sang songs of unrequited love and its torments. Gotfried von Strassburg led the way of the romantic writers with his epic love story of *Tristan and Isolde*, which does reasonably well as unrequited love right up until the bit where Isolde loses her resolve and the ability to *Just Say No* and the adultery happens.

Adultery takes courtly love one step further by actually consummating the relationship. The trick is, of course, not to get caught.

Adultery

Adultery was rarely grounds for divorce, although it did feature in court cases where either the husband or wife had strayed and been caught. An adulterous wife would most likely find herself severely beaten or worse. It was a worrying situation for a husband, because if his wife did go off and have sex with someone else, it might be because he was failing in his duty to satisfy her in the marital bed himself, and no one wants to admit to that. Generally, a sound beating and being told off by the court would fix that, though. Maybe.

Nevertheless, husbands and other women both accused women of being adulterers and took them to court for chastisement or retribution. It was one thing to accuse someone of adultery, but if one hoped for results, one needed proof. Even in cases of adultery, it was usually the woman involved who shouldered the blame, regardless of whether the man in question was a known fornicator or just of poor morals.

Agnes Brignall of St Michael le Belfrey

Agnes Brignall was living in a suburb of York in 1432 when she married one John Herford. Or she says that she did. One rather lengthy court case regarding Agnes hinges around whether the marriage actually happened and whether she had committed adultery with not only him, but a number of other men, and that there was no contract of marriage. And that she was, in fact, suspect. Many witnesses were called for on each side, but as the case wore on, the usual practice of finding out whose witnesses were more reliable started to come into play. It seemed a typical case, but with some interesting details.

The gentleman in question, John Herford *alias* John Smyth, who was supposed to have made a contract of marriage with Agnes and had certainly been having a lot of sex with her, got many friends to swear that he was out of town the whole time buying a horse for his boss, that he had sworn no marriage at all, and that Agnes's witnesses were adulterers themselves and not to be trusted. John's witnesses seem to be contradicting themselves as to whether he was buying or selling a horse at the fair, which they should know, but at any rate, a horse was definitely involved.

Agnes's witnesses even described the day, the date and the time of day, and the location, right down to what all the parties were wearing and what fish was eaten for dinner on that day, as well as the alleged marriage vows, but to no avail. Character assassination was hard at work on John's side, hoping to discredit Agnes's witnesses, one of whom was her own sister.

Isabel Henryson of Bootham

The case takes an interesting twist when the testimony of Agnes's sister Isabel is called into question as an unreliable witness because she is accused of being an adulteress. Isabel is described as being aged thirty years and more, the natural blood sister of Agnes and currently living with her. The records reveal:

> *Asked further, he says that he often heard it said by several men and women, residence of the city of York and its suburbs, that John Willerdby, a married man, held the same Isabel for many years in the embrace of adultery and procreated three or four children by her.*

Whilst what Isabel does or doesn't do with whom in her own time has absolutely nothing to do with the case itself, but by proving that she is a woman of base intentions and morals, it makes her testimony in her sister's court case less believable. The fact that Alice's witnesses can describe small details about the marriage vows like what she and the couple were wearing, what

the weather was like that day, and what they had for dinner is over-ruled by another witness who doesn't even know how many children she has, is ridiculous. What was the outcome? Who knows? The court then got distracted with the unfortunate Isabel.

As far as adultery goes, the most usual suspects were the clergy who certainly preyed on the wives of other men in their parishes. We know some took advantage of their single household staff, but others preferred other men's wives whom they would never be required to marry.

Katherine Walrond of Waddesdon and Elizabeth Godday of Waddesdon

From the church court in the archdeaconry of Buckingham, we meet Elizabeth and Katherine who have their local chaplain on their minds. From the late fifteenth century court records, we read:

> *Visitation 1495. Waddesdon. Elizabeth Godday called Katherine Walrond a whore alleging that she incited Sir Thomas Couley, chaplain, to commit adultery. She appeared and denied the charge. She purged herself and was let off.*

Although she was let off, appearing in court on charges like these made her a slightly suspect woman. What drove Elizabeth to accuse Katherine is unknown, but it may have been that she had been spurned by the chaplain herself and fancied that he had his roving eye on Katherine. Perhaps she was an ex-lover of his. We all know that hell hath no fury like a woman scorned. It may also have been that the accusation was true, but there was no real proof, Elizabeth being a woman and all, and her word carrying no real weight. Had a man accused her of adultery, even with no proof, it may have been another story altogether.

In the Name of God

Priests often pleaded innocent to being the instigators, citing their holiness. As we already know, however, clergy were not usually the innocent victims of seduction, but the ones doing the seducing. Priests sometimes were able to convince their victims that their very personal holiness excused them from the sin of adultery; since all sex was unholy, it mattered not whether a woman was married or not.

This was very much the view of Pierre Clergue, who singlehandedly caused a number of married women to break their vows to their respective husbands. Pierre was extremely active in a small French village in the very early fourteenth century. His worst episode occurred when he first deflowered a young virgin, married her off to someone else, and then continued to have adulterous sex with her.

Grazide Rives of Montaillou

Grazide was born in the French village of Montaillou in 1298 or 1299 and had the misfortune of catching the eye of a priest who wanted to have sex with her and also having a mother who didn't care. Around 1313, the priest Pierre Clergue, who, by all accounts, seemed quite unable to refrain from illicit sex and just keep it in his breeches, waited until Grazide's mother was at work in the fields harvesting corn and hunted out the girl whilst she was home alone. Later, as her story came before religious enquiries of the Cathars, we learn what happened to her.

> *Seven years ago or thereabouts, in summer, the priest Pierre Clergue came to my mother's house whilst she was out harvesting, and was very pressing. "Allow me to know you carnally." And I said, "All right." At that time I was a virgin. I think I was fourteen or fifteen years old. He deflowered me in the barn in which we kept the straw. But it wasn't a rape at all. After that, he continued to know me*

> *carnally until the following January. It always took place in my mother's ostal, she knew about it and was consenting.*

So, her mother knew and apparently approved of her daughter being used for sex by a much older man who had already had a string of lovers in the same village. What a great mother. It gets worse for Grazide because although she is told that everything is as it should be, it doesn't seem to occur to her that this is not how a normal marriage functioned.

> *After that, in January, the priest gave me as wife to my late husband Pierre Lizier; and after he had given me to this man, the priest continued to know me carnally, frequently, during the remaining four years of my husband's life. And my husband knew about it, and was consenting. Sometimes he would ask me, "Has the priest done it with you?" and I would answer, "Yes." And my husband would say, "As far as the priest is concerned, all right. But don't you go having other men."*

The manipulation of such a young girl is just horrible, but worse is that the priest appeared to talk her into sex at the start with very little resistance so that, as with the victims of most sexual predators, the girl was quite willing and saw nothing wrong with what she was doing.

To make matters worse, when she was married at fifteen or sixteen, her new husband permitted the ongoing abuse as long as it was confined to just the priest and to no other man. Being traded off as a sex toy to another man so her husband can get in good with God is just one of the things that a young girl might face. I mean, what choice does she have? None that she knows of.

By 1320, Grazide was just nineteen when she called the whole thing off, citing her lack of desire for Pierre. Lack of desire made what they were doing sinful. Whether she genuinely felt that or not, she finally decided to stand up for herself. Better late than

never. Unlike other lovers of Pierre, she appeared to not go back once she had closed that door.

Good for her.

Bewitchment

Women, being the sex-crazed hussies that they were because of their cold natures, or so it seemed to the imaginings of very concerned men, were at risk of being accused of making unwilling men desire to couple with them through devious means. This was often accompanied with finger-pointing and name-calling.

Women might be charged with bewitching a man against his will, and not in a good, romantic, courtly kind of way, but a straight out bewitched-with-a-spell kind of way. We only know of women who had affairs by the ones who were found out and punished. In exceptionally rare cases, the wives were not conducting private affairs secretly, but actively running amok with little regard for their husband or their good reputation, as we see in the interesting court case of Joan Beverley.

Joan Beverley of London

The church courts in London in 1481 heard a complaint against one Joan who was most definitely, maybe, probably not getting enough with her husband and took it outside her martial home.

> *St Sepulchre. Joan Beverley, or Lessell, or Cowcross, is a witch, and she asked two accomplices to work together, so that Robert Stantone and another Gentle-born of Gray's Inn should love her and no other, and they committed adultery with her, and as it is said, fought for her, and one almost killed the other, and her husband does not dare stay with her on account of these two men. She is a common whore, and a procuress, and she wants to poison men.*

That's quite a lot of name-calling in such a small paragraph. Something's going on for sure. Some kind of terrifying love triangle which excludes her actual husband and involves not only one, but two other men. It's unfortunate that he is the only legitimate sex partner of hers and also the only one who is not willing to go anywhere near her. Either way, Joan whatever-her-name-is was the very epitome of a foul temptress in the eyes of fifteenth-century London.

What a strumpette.

Chapter 10

Strumpettes and Where to Find Them

Prostitution as a Sin

Prostitution was tricky. On one hand, a woman becoming a prostitute and selling her body for money was sinning on a number of moral levels, but some of the time, it was seen as not that bad, really. It was definitely better than rape as the woman was consenting and also got paid, and if everyone was happy, then what was the harm? Pierre Vidal, who was a priest in Ax-les-Thermes in Medieval France discussed this with a learned colleague one day.

> *Yesterday, I was going from Tarascon to Ax-les-Thermes with two mules laden with corn. I met a priest and we went along together. As we were going down the slope after the village of Laussur, the conversation turned to prostitutes. If you found a prostitute, said the priest, and agreed with her on a price, and then slept with her, do you think you would be committing a mortal sin? Finally, I answered, "No, I don't think so."*

The discussion hinged not so much on the woman's lack of morals, but focused on the transaction being a financial one, that of the prostitute providing a paid-for service. If it was also agreeable to both parties, then in the eyes of God, how could such an arrangement be ungodly? It was surely no different than hiring a woman to provide a service like any other service. There should be no distinction between a woman hired for laundry, or

for sewing, or for brewing beer, and one hired for a sexual union. If one party was not happy with the arrangement, only *then* did it become a sin.

There's some quality logic for you.

Grazide Lizier of Montaillou

Grazide, a French woman, was in agreeance with this theory and was most definite about this. When questioned about having had willing sex with a priest in the past, she replied:

> *In those days it pleased me, and it pleased the priest, that he should know me carnally, and be known by me; and so I did not think that I was sinning, and neither did he. But now, with him, it does not please me anymore. And so now, if he knew me carnally, I should think it a sin!*

It certainly sounded like there was far more sinning going on than the recommended none-at-all, especially for a priest.

Not everyone agreed with this rather flexible logic of sinning. Some people adopted a more zero-tolerance approach, which, whilst taking the high ground morally, was quite likely to deprive a woman with no other financial options into even further financial difficulty. If she had nothing more to sell other than herself, and then was deprived of that income, only begging and bleakest poverty remained.

In spite of this, France felt it had the answer. In a somewhat optimistic attempt to rid the entire country of loose women, Louis IX took a bold step. In 1254, he passed a law removing all the prostitutes from the country. If that wasn't far-reaching enough, they were to be stripped of their goods, their money, and their clothes. You may already see how this was doomed to failure. Finding alternate means of income when one is in a foreign country, naked, and without money just seems a recipe for disaster, if not a rash of clothing theft by the women who were ousted.

By the early 1400s, the general population of Paris reached around seventy-five thousand. Three thousand of those were known prostitutes. As the calendar flipped to 1500, Rome counted seven thousand, whilst Venice recorded over eleven-and-a-half thousand out of a population of one hundred and fifty thousand. Dijon, by comparison, had a measly hundred. Venice, then, was party central for the single man. Or the religious one who was not terribly big on practicing what he preached.

Reasons for Prostitution

Money. Money was, for the most part, the reason. Most women turned to prostitution because they were poor and had no other means of survival. Others had been unable to find good marriages due to their previous loose behaviour or outright slander, making them unmarriageable.

Finding work as a servant was difficult if a woman was of dubious character. A ruined reputation also made a woman a target for sex she hadn't asked for because she was seen as *spoilt* anyway. Some women became owners of brothels, stepped back from doing the work themselves, and employed a number of other women to do the work for them. Some worked from home. Some even became procuresses and offered their own household servants or their own daughters for sale.

Margery Tubbe of Iver

Occasionally, the archdeaconry visited more rural areas, and in fifteenth-century Buckingham, we find a certain lady who did not appear to be a prostitute herself, but rather was the middle-man for her own daughter and anyone who was willing to pay.

> *1496. Iver. Margery Tubbe because a procuress between her and her own daughter and various men. She appeared and purged herself and was dismissed.*

It appears that the daughter of Margery who was doing the actual prostituting was not required to attend court or plead her own case. She appeared to not require a punishment, and it isn't recorded whether the unfortunate daughter was a willing participant in the arrangements or whether she had absolutely no say whatsoever. My guess is that she was choiceless.

Forced Prostitution

To the modern person, it must seem that prostitution was a terrible life, and indeed it was. Poor women forced into this kind of life with no other option were taken advantage of and often beaten or injured by clients and brothel owners. Other servant girls were, unwillingly, we assume, forced into it by their household employers.

The Servant Girl of Nicholas de Prese of Southhampton

Such was the lot of an unnamed woman from Southampton whose story is alluded to in the borough memoranda of 1482:

> *Memorandum that Nicholas de Prese, cordwainer, and his wife for certain offences or promoting illicit sex between a captain of a Venetian galley and a servant girl staying with the said Nicholas and his wife in which offences they colluded.*

There appears to be no actual charge or fine levied against Nicholas or his unnamed wife or any further note on whether there was a penalty incurred, only that it was made note of. The servant girl also remains unnamed, as if she is not particularly important, either. No mention of whether this was an isolated incident or whether the girl was regularly farmed out for financial gain. It appears quite important to mention that the galley

was Venetian and that the man the de Prese's entertained was a captain.

Court records were weirdly specific at times.

Isabel Lane of London and Margaret Hathewyk of London

Other records are a bit more specific about the young women who were forced into prostitution. The borough courts of London tell a sad story of a girl who clearly had no other option than to put up with the men thrust upon her by the older woman who most likely promised her honest household work. Household it was. Honest, it certainly wasn't.

> *1439. The jurors say that a certain Margaret Hathewyk often...in the parish of St Edmund in Lombard Street procured a young girl named Isabel Lane for certain Lombards and other men, unknown, which Isabel was deflowered against her will in the said Margaret's house and elsewhere for certain sums of money paid to the said Margaret, and further the said Margaret took the said Isabel to the common stews on the banks of the Thames in Surrey against her will for immoral purposes with a certain unknown gentleman on four occasions against her will.*

What is heart-breaking is that the young girl was in no way a willing part of this new life she had thrust upon her, but since she was no longer a virgin and was seen to be a common whore, her chances of a marriage, good or otherwise, were extremely unlikely. Where she was procured from and why she stayed are not mentioned, but again, like the daughter of Margery Tubbe, she appeared to have no other option available to her.

Els von Eystett of Nördlingen and Barbara Tarschenfeindin of Nördlingen

A third and equally heart-breaking case is that of a poor kitchen maid named Els. Els von Eystett was a German girl in the fifteenth century who was working as a kitchen maid at a brothel. She had been forced into seeing clients very much against her will and had fallen pregnant as a result.

The establishment was run by Lienhart Fryermut and Barbara Tarschenfeindin, and Barbara wasted no time in taking care of the situation when she found out. Els was about twenty weeks pregnant when she was forced by Barbara to drink a *certain preparation* which caused her to abort her baby.

If that was not awful enough, Barbara then put Els back to work in the brothel a few days later and swore her to secrecy. If only it was as easy as that. Women talk, and prostitutes were no different, so it wasn't long before the rest of the women working for Barbara and Lienhart were discussing the situation. Clients even began to whisper of how it was possible that Els, previously large, was now suddenly so small.

Barbel von Esslingen, who also worked for Barbara at the brothel, said she had seen a male child laid out on a bench in Els's room whilst Els herself lay on the bed in pain. After voicing this to the other women, she earned herself a hasty exit from the brothel as Barbara, who had the brothel's reputation to consider, sent her elsewhere. It was too late. Word had gotten out. In 1471, the council of Nördlingen began an investigation into the rumours of improper goings-on of Barbara and Lienhart. One can only hope that there was justice for Els, but the records do not say.

Redemption

Once entrenched in this line of work, it was almost impossible to leave it. Prostitutes had very few options to redeem themselves and become honest wives and mothers, but in 1198, the optimistic Pope Innocent III declared that marrying a whore in order to reform her was an act of charity. They *could* marry, if they could find a husband.

On the whole, it was all a bit unlikely.

A Great Escape

The best way to escape the lifestyle of a prostitute was to repent and join a religious order. This was, by far, the most church-approved method of leaving the life of sin behind, potential husbands being a little scarce on the convent's grounds and all. Houses and religious orders, like the fourteenth-century Order of the Repentant Sisters of St Catherine in Montpellier, offered a life which conveniently kept the lately-converted, ex-sinning women away from other, more serious nuns in case their devotion was lacking in sincerity. No, really.

At the Order of the Repentant Sisters of St Catherine, confession was a relaxed once-a-month affair instead of a more regular every Sunday or daily arrangement. As a retirement home option for women who were too old to earn a decent living as a prostitute, it was quite a good one, and stories around the table after dinner may have been well worth eavesdropping on. The hot subject of Sins I've Committed and with Whom may have provided much merriment, but not a heap of devout contemplation.

The exact amount of genuine repentance in the Order of the Repentant Sisters quite probably varied on a sliding scale of Not Very Much to Maybe Just a Little Bit. The registering of a new arrival may have been a charade well worth seeing. The following is not a transcript of any actual new arrival.

Sister Agnes of the Order of The Repentant Sisters of St Catherine is busy filling in a wine order for the feast of the Purification next week. She was going to need a tun of it if she was going to purify her girls. There is a knock at the door, and a hesitant older woman of obvious dubious character steps out of the shadows...

Sister Agnes: *Can I help you?*

Visitor: *Yes, uh, maybe. I'd like to join the Order.*

Sister Agnes eyes her suspiciously

Sister Agnes: *You're a prostitute, aren't you?*

Visitor: *No. I mean, uh...yes. Well, I was.*

Sister Agnes: *I see.*

Visitor: *But I want to leave all that behind. I'm feeling... um...quite repentant and all that. I'm...uh...really sorry?*

Sister Agnes: *I see.*

Visitor: *Only I was told that if I'm truly sorry, then I can join the order and live here for the rest of my days with food and lodging for free and...uh...pray? And...things like that?*

Sister Agnes: *You don't sound terribly sorry. Have you truly repented?*

Visitor: *Oh yes! I'm probably deeply regretful about some of the things I did. I'm sure of it. Deeply regretful. I'm feeling...uh...remorseful?*

Sister Agnes: *Hmm. Tell me some of the things you regret.*

Visitor: *Well. There was that time I had my fur-lined hood confiscated by the authorities in Paris. I regret that. And that time I got busted in Nice and they took my silver belt from me. It was really nice, too. Deeply regretful about my belt. And there was the time that hot monk from St Bernard's asked for the special and then slipped out without paying me. He was super cute. I'd like to regret a bit more with him.*

Sister Agnes: *Brother Andrew? You fornicated with Brother Andrew!*

Visitor: *Oh! Um... Well... I... regret...*

Sister Agnes: *Oh, he'll be so glad to see you! Come on in and let's get you all signed up. Friday is "fish day," if you*

know what I mean, and Andy's out the back taking a look at Sister Ethel's plumbing at the moment. You're going to love it here.

Where to Find Them

In most cities and towns, women of this sort were usually relegated to certain parts. It was far better to have the strumpettes gathered neatly in one area than have them just living wherever they might choose. One might have a neighbour who was convicted of wantonness, and no one wanted that. Courts continually heard from concerned citizens about the suspicious goings-on in the neighbourhood, especially where women lived alone, were widowed, or had a lively social life, the participants of which were mostly men.

Gossipy villagers didn't make these women's lives easier in the least and were quite prone to finger-pointing and name-calling. So, where might we find these women? Let's make a mental map, shall we?

France

Starting with Paris between 1226 and 1270, Louis IX set aside nine streets in the Beaubourg Quartier. Nine streets seems quite specific, but depending on how long those nine streets were, a lot of establishments might be run there.

Bratislava

Bratislava in Western Slovakia had a fifteenth-century brothel helpfully located near the southern city gate, close to the Hungarian and Austrian borders. Amusingly, it was also known locally as the fisherman's gate, even if it was located nowhere near the sea. It was a gateway to another kind of fishing. After 1432, the city put its foot down and moved the business out of

the city centre. Later still, in 1439, the women were moved even further out of town and into the suburbs to the east.

Buda, Hungary

Houses of prostitution here were called *Frauenhauses*, and the women who worked there called *gutted Fräulein*, which is not really a compliment in anyone's book. In 1472, the Council of Bolzano took the step of establishing a place for prostitutes to live and then charged them rent equating to £70 a year to live there. The brothel owner was sworn in by the mayor every two years or so, which is nice. The people running the city ought to be in touch with its key infrastructure players, should they not? The Frauenhaus housed twelve to thirteen workers who boarded, and it was located not far from the hangman's house. Whether this acted as any kind of deterrent to the behaviour of the working women is pure speculation. Maybe those who worked with death day in and day out needed professional relief more than those in other trades. Maybe it was a convenient stop in the last wishes department.

Valencia, Spain

By the very start of the sixteenth century, travellers in Valencia would find prostitutes in their own little neighbourhood. In 1502, Antione de Lalaing, who was passing through at the time and certainly not stopping or doing a nose count, couldn't help but notice:

> *...like a little town, surrounded by walls and a single gate, with a gate keeper. Inside in around three or four streets, there were small houses with richly dressed women in silk and damask (between two hundred and three hundred women altogether) plying their trade. The municipality set the fees at four dineros, and the little enclave of prostitution had two doctors who visited the women on a weekly basis.*

Clearly, these women were at the higher end of the socio-economic spectrum, able to afford beautiful silk and gorgeous damask gowns. With such a large number of women working there, it was no wonder that more than one doctor was required to keep an eye on them. Aside from the violence bestowed on them by the clientele, there was the matter of sexually transmitted diseases and infections as well as general good health issues to oversee.

Sopron, Hungary

Sopron is located on the Austrian border which, it must be said, is pretty handy for catching the passing trade from both countries. Most of the brothels in Sopron date back to between 1330 to 1380 and were located on Rose Street at the northern end of the city. Later, further brothels opened up near the water and along trade routes. No snickering.

London, England

Borough High Street in London itself was home to a brothel owned by a clergyman before it was unceremoniously moved across the river to the prostitute district in Southwark. Some streets today still carry the names given to them in earlier times. Cock Lane springs instantly to mind. In the fifteenth century, long-suffering Londoners once again brought a petition through the courts to ban *strumpettes and idil women* from hanging out in the city. Many cities permitted prostitution, but Southwark in England tried to restrict their business to shorter working days on holy days and not at all during church services. Women were forbidden to pull a man by the gown or his hood into a brothel and were told that he must enter of his own free will. To violate this rule incurred a hefty fine of twenty shillings.

By 1381, the stewes were the property of the rather enterprising Lord Mayor of London, Sir William Walworth, who imported a slew of prostitutes who were Flemish and had golden tresses and full figures. Inns such as The Bell and The Swan were known to be

establishments where more than food and drink was available. Later, Westminster was the not-so-proud home of a brothel called the Maidenshead, which was quite well known to the Benedictine monks who were keen patrons in 1447.

Eventually, King Henry VIII put his foot down about the lawlessness and licentiousness going on across the Thames and finally closed down the Southwark stewes in 1546. Not easily deterred, the women and their pimps and brothel owners simply moved to different parts of the city. Cokkes Lane, Petticoat Lane, Popkirtle Lane, and Gropecunte Lane in Cheapside are streets that still exist today which allude to the sex trade carried out there. Gropecunte Lane seems a shocking thing to name a street to our modern ears, but in Medieval England, the C word was the everyday term for a woman's privy parts, even in reasonably polite society. Only now does it have unseemly and impolite connotations.

The Establishments

Bathhouses or *stewes* were a favourite place to work for ladies who charged for their company.

Medieval people did bathe more frequently that usually imagined, and, in fact, bathhouses were not just mere bathing establishments, but places where meals and wine might be served in the tub itself, along with live music. Tubs were large enough for dual bathing and had fabric canopies, which was a recipe for sinful situations if ever there was one.

Manuscript image of a bath house from the Psalter Hours.

Dated 1315-1325, Ghent. Walters Ex Libris, Manuscript W.82 folio100r.

Many of these establishments were genuine bath houses. They were actual places where bathing might occur. Much like our massage parlours of today, some operated for their intended and advertised purposes, whilst some added that optional extra.

Many paintings and manuscripts of bathhouses of this type show scantily clad or naked women bathing alongside men to the tunes of lute players. I can't imagine the heat from the baths was particularly good for their precious instruments, but I can imagine that the pay was reasonably good. Discretion, of course, was as important as the ability to string a tune together in a pleasing manner whilst turning a blind eye to the goings-on under the canopy.

Faire Play

Although around the world these strumpettes were regulated to certain districts, of course, the women who worked there often failed to adhere to the regulations to take advantage of public events like fairs where they might ply their trade and hopefully gain new customers. As you can imagine, decent people everywhere were horrified at this gross breech of form, and the authorities were called to deal with the women who dared to leave their designated areas. The court from the Fair records the prostitute round-up which took place at St Ives in England.

> *1287. Ralph de Armeston, his companion, and all the bailiffs are ordered to take all the bodies of the said prostitutes and all the bodies of all the other prostitutes, wherever they are found within the bounds and perimeters of the fair, and bring them to the court and guard them securely...*

It's comforting to know that in addition to the prostitutes they had, they rounded up the other ones as well. And guarded them securely. I'll bet there was a bit of a disorderly queue for *that* job.

Prostitutes and the Law

In England, ordinances were drawn up to protect the rights of the women who worked at brothels so that they might not be taken advantage of. Fines were levied against owners doing the wrong thing. Apart from selling other people's sexual favours for money, which was, in itself, the wrong thing, brothel-keepers or stewe-holders were not permitted to keep single women against their will, which attracted a fine of a hundred shillings. Or married women. Or nuns. The penalty for allowing a nun or a married woman was a mere twelve pence, so it wasn't much of a deterrent. Also, no pregnant women. Or those women who had the burning sickness. No prize for guessing what that was.

Furthermore, brothels in England at that time could only be run by men or a married couple and not by a single woman. Single women who sold themselves at their own home were liable to be fined by the court for improper behaviour and sexual incontinence, but a brothel couldn't force a woman to live on-site if she chose to go home again at the end of the day. To do so risked a twenty-shilling fine.

Margery Grey of York

This was the case of one Margery Grey from York in 1483.

> *Cherrylips. Memorandum that 12 day of May…the whole parish of St Martin in Micklegate came before my Lord Mayor and complained Margery Grey, otherwise called Cherrylips, that she was a woman ill disposed of her body to whom ill desposed men resort to much to the annoyance of her neighbours.*

But not to the annoyance of the ones who visit her and her sexy red lips.

Getting satisfaction from the courts was difficult. Women may be brought before the courts, prosecuted, and fined, but other times, the authorities turned a blind eye or actively took bribes from the women themselves. From the fourteenth century, Calendar of Plea and Memoranda Rolls of the City of London, we find exactly that. Not only were women giving up bribes for protection, they were caught doing so:

> *1344. The jury further found that the beadle of Farringdon Without took bribes from disorderly women in his ward to protect them in their practices.*

Call me suspicious, but I expect some of those bribes involved things other than money. As well as the money.

Raynauda of Melius

In other countries, prostitution occurred through different approaches. Pezenas in France took a more holistic approach. In the fifteenth century, the town itself owned the brothel, and the woman running it, Raynauda of Melius, became the brothel farmer, who was the intermediator. She organised the running of the establishment, taking a share of the profits for herself and paying a certain amount to the town. Usually the brothel farmers were other women, but as the fifteenth century was drawing to a close, men replaced women in the managerial roles, much to the unhappiness of the workers. The Royal Court at Toulouse

heard a complaint from the local sex workers that hinged on the uncaring attitude of their new male boss. The women felt they were overworked and that he was behaving no better than a common procurer.

This tells us a number of things about what was going on with brothels at that time in France. The workers were reasonably organised, so much so that they felt able to make a formal legal complaint against the person who employed them, which is a bit of a big call, even today. It also tells us that there was an acceptable workload for the industry and that to constantly over-reach this was not okay.

It also tells us that the women making the complaint expected to be heard with seriousness and not laughed out of the courtroom, and that they had hopes that their complaint would achieve some kind of result.

The Church Weighs In

The church, as much as they denounced men fornicating with any women other than their own wives, recognised that single men needed an outlet for their hot natures and agreed that prostitutes were an evil necessity. They weren't happy about it, by a long shot, and sermons advised that these kinds of women were to be strenuously avoided.

Ironically, churchmen were also not above being heavily involved in the industry in quite a hands-on way. A brothel in Dijon, France lists twenty percent of its clients as churchmen. What I particularly like is that not only did the churchman frequent the establishment, the woman who ran the place kept some kind of ledger, noting who the clients were. Blackmail material much?

The Winchester Geese

Taking that extra step further, some churchmen took the opportunity to become owners themselves.

It's recorded that the Bishop of Winchester received regular rent from the brothels of Southwark stewes across the river Thames in London. His ladies were colloquially known as his *Winchester geese*. The enterprising bishop organised that his estate managers would not only collect the rent but conduct weekly site inspections of the women's quarters and take a personal interest in any money owed.

The cherry on the top is that, in a document drawn up in the fifteenth century, the *Ordinances Touching the Government of the Stewholders in Southwark under the Direction of the Bishop of Winchester,* the bishop not only sets out thirty-six regulations for those working there, he also set fines for anyone breaking those rules. Talk about hedging one's bets.

It's a quiet Monday, and all is quiet at the brothel. The owner of the brothel, Alyce, is checking over the books for the month as Father Mark enters and looks around.

Alyce: *Father Mark! How lovely to see you! What can we do for you today?*

Father Mark: *I was just passing by. Look, you haven't seen the Bishop anywhere, have you? He said he was coming down to check you out, but I don't see him...*

Alyce: *Room five. With Margy.*

Father Mark: *I'll just be on my wa...wait, what?*

Alyce: *He arrived about half an hour ago. Room five with Margy.*

Father Mark: *I think there must be some kind of misunderstanding.*

Alyce, flicking through register: *No here it is. Arrived 9:30 AM. Room five, Margy.*

Father Mark: *Is that a list of your clients?*

Alyce: *Of course. Names, prices, time of visit. All perfectly above board and proper for the records. Brother Charles,*

room three, Mary. Father Edmund, room six, Elle. John Roper, room four, Alice. Bishop Sebastian, room five, Margy.

The Bishop appears, tucking himself in.

Bishop: *Oh Mark! I was...uh...just inspecting the rooms. Everything seems to be fine, and I'll just collect the rent and we'll be off then.*

Father Mark: *They have a register. A register! Names. Dates. Times.*

Alyce: *All proper and above board.*

Bishop: *May I see it? No? Well then, about the rent...*

Alyce: *Yes? The rent?*

Alyce taps the ledger suggestively.

Bishop: *Well. I see. We...might not need it this month, perhaps...and everything seems to be in order...no violations...I'll see myself out.*

Alyce: *See you tomorrow, then...it's Two for Tuesdays! Bring a friend for free!*

Clientele

The Prodigal Son at a Brothel.

Manuscript. Ludwig XV 9 (8ß3.MR.179), fol. 1060. Getty Images.

What kind of man might the lady who works in a stew expect to find as her client? Desperate, single men? No. Not really. The ladies attracted a diverse range of customers. Single men for sure, but also many wayward husbands and professionals made good use of them too.

There is a story of a certain doctor who was called to treat a woman who worked at the stewes and

whilst he was there, he looked accidentally through a hole in the wall, and was aghast to see his learned, married friend resting in the arms of a sweet young thing post-coitus. The friend in question was reprimanded sternly and returned to his wife with pleas not to return and disgrace his wife and family with his folly.

Socially Aware Prostitutes

Just because a woman earned her living providing sexual favours didn't mean that she hadn't any social conscious at all. Many women who worked in a brothel were also a part of the greater society and involved themselves with community projects.

In Paris, the city sex workers banded together and made a large charitable donation to the cathedral of Notre Dame. The funds were to provide a stained-glass window in one of the chapels. This was a daring move. Other guilds had made similar donations, and the windows which depicted religious scenes often had a market to identify the guild or workshop who had provided the funds for it. Naturally, a stained-glass window funded by sex workers was a something to consider, and consider it they did. Eventually, the bishop refused to accept the money on the grounds that it was tainted by sin.

He did give it a lot of thought, though.

Industry Regulations

A text of ordinances from England dating to the 12th century and reiterated again in the 14th century gives some rules and regulations for prostitutes and brothel keepers. One states the following about women who chose to live externally, but work in-house:

> *The women that are at common brothel be seen every day what they are, and a woman that lives by her body [be*

> *allowed] to come and go, as long as she pays her duty as old custom is.*

There were guidelines for the hours worked and for the wages to be expected. In other words, the women who lived outside of the brothels or stewes themselves but worked in brothels paid a fee to the brothel owner to conduct her work in her establishment. In fourteenth-century London, this amount was twelve pence each week.

Other industry regulations ensured, like our unions today, that the women might not be taken advantage or of being overworked. With that in mind, we have a court record of a legal complaint made against a *certain woman* who had been keeping prostitutes and treating them badly. How bad can it be, you might wonder, with trepidation? Beatings? Long hours? Unsuitable clients? I know you're wondering. I'll tell you.

The hideous, terrible, awful thing she was doing to these poor women was...she had been working the women at...and I'm sorry to shock the sensitive amongst us...working at...*spinning wool* in their spare time.

This was such a scandalous thing to do to a prostitute! Totally not acceptable. Spinning wool was a job for honest women and honest daughters and honest wives. Earning extra money from an honest job was simply not an optional extra for a prostitute. For modern people, this is a slightly perplexing way of thinking. Surely this could only be a good thing? Today we think that by giving a woman with no other way to earn a living a good skill or a trade, we are lifting her out of her situation, hoping to keep her off the streets, and, indeed, out of the whole line of selling her body to put food on the table and a roof over her head. Attitudes were very different to prostitutes then.

Markers

Whilst attitudes were different to prostitutes then than they are now, not all of the feelings were of pity and despair. Some feelings were of envy and jealousy. How can that be? Surely not! I'll explain.

Some high-end prostitutes earned quite a good living and were able to afford to dress better than their social superiors. They had no husbands to tell them to tone it down a bit, and they could often afford luxury items which were above the reach of honest women who were expected to dress well, but modestly. In these cases, they might, and often did, out-dress their social superiors. This was something the rest of society found appalling. One might accidentally talk to one in error. Worse than that was the actual case of the unfortunate Queen Margaret of Provence who gave the kiss of peace to a woman at church who, horrifyingly, was not a good woman at all. How was she to tell? It was all a bit embarrassing.

Sumptuary Laws

Many sumptuary laws were put in place in an effort to limit the amount of finery a woman might have. In an amusing conflict of interest, other laws begrudgingly agreed that a certain amount of bling was necessary as part of the tools of the trade. On the whole, law-makers had limited success, and it was certainly only a matter of being punished if caught. As early as 1162, statutes complied by the council at Arles forbade prostitutes from wearing veils and actively encouraged honest women to snatch the veils from their heads whilst they were wearing them. An honest woman would most certainly wear a veil and most likely a wimple as well to protect from the elements and keep herself demure, so to have one's veil removed by another woman in public was a grave insult paramount to calling her a common whore.

Selected regulations imposed by English Sumptuary Laws included:

- 1355 – Statute regulating the dress of prostitutes.
- 1399 (or 1388) – Regulating apparel suitable to every man's distinct rank and quality. Listed in the Parliamentary History of England and Knighton's chronicle.
- 1439–40 – Sumptuary regulation for the dress of prostitutes (a repeat of the clearly not-very-successful 1355 statute).

Select regulations imposed by French Sumptuary Laws aimed at prostitutes included more specifics:

- 1360 – Prostitutes are forbidden to wear embroidery of any kind, pearls, gilt or silver buttons and squirrel fur edges on their clothes.
- 1427 – Paris forbade gold and silver buttons, buckles, belts, pearls and furred robes.
- Paris also forbade excesses such as shoulder capes, coral rosaries, and books of hours which had silver clasps.

The fact that laws were repeatedly passed shows how ignored and unsuccessful they were. Quite frankly, what fear of the fiery chasms of forever was there for the sin of vanity if a woman's line of work was sure to send her to hell, anyway? She may as well look nice going.

Jeanette le Petite of Paris

Penalties were often the confiscation or removal of the offending item or items. In 1427, a secular court in Paris publicly gave a certain Jeanette le Petite a good talking to for overdressing and looking like any other honest woman. Her linen sleeves were torn off, the train of her gown cut completely off, and her expensive silver belt donated to a hospital.

Less than thirty years later, Dijon in France allowed prostitutes to wear nicer clothes if they could afford them, and in Avignon, silks and furs were permitted. It was salacious. It was scandalous.

Specific Clothing Examples

Many attempts were made to inflict women with specific kinds of clothing requirements so that they might be easily recognisable and not mistaken for decent wives and daughters. England tried to ban anyone who wasn't a fine upstanding model of virtue from wearing nice dress accessories as well. Women who were known to be prostitutes in 1353 London were instructed:

> *It was ordained at the insistence of the people of London that no woman who was known to be a prostitute should wear a hood unless it were striped, nor should she wear furs, nor lined garments.*

If they weren't known beforehand, they certainly would stand out from the crowd in their striped hoods and quickly become known. Both in the literal and biblical senses. Although not the intended result, it was pretty much free advertising. Other towns and times had their own unique ways of singling out these women with their optimistic dress restrictions, which were also utterly ignored.

These included:

- Striped hood – London, 1353 (if a hood was worn at all, it was to be a striped one so that she would adequately stand out)
- Yellow hood – London (conflicting with the striped hood of 1353)
- Red knot on the shoulder – several French cities
- White clothes – Toulouse, Parma
- Yellow and blue cloaks – Leipzig, Germany
- Red caps – Bern, Zurich
- Cloak of Prostitution – Paris, 1250

Contraceptives for Sex Workers

It comes as no real surprise that the women who most wanted to prevent pregnancy were prostitutes. Prostitutes were definitely the women in the most high-risk category of Women Likely to Get Pregnant, and they had an exceptionally keen interest in not doing so and remaining open for business. The sheer number of prostitutes made this an important consideration. Sex workers had all the usual options about not being pregnant open to them that we have seen in previous chapters, but some people had extra ideas about what prostitutes might be doing or the reasons they failed to fall pregnant.

It was no great secret that St Augustine was not particularly prostitute-friendly, and he had quite a bit to say about the evils of it and the women themselves. They vexed him, especially, not only for their lifestyle and their line of work, but for their suspected contraceptive taking. He was quite sure about this because few prostitutes were also mothers.

St Augustine wrote about it in his work *Against Secundinus*. He was not the only one who looked suspiciously at women who had a lot of coitus and, yet, very few offspring. Others also has ideas about this. William of Conches was one of them, and he was certain he knew how this came about:

> *Prostitutes after frequent acts of coitus have their womb clogged with dirt and the villosities in which the semen should be retained are covered over; that is why, like greased marble, the womb immediately rejects what it receives.*

Magnus, too, mentioned this in his *Secrets of Women*. He had another theory about why coitus didn't produce the usual resulting pregnancy when there was so much of it. He felt that the large volume of male seed provided from the equally large volume of men mixed together in the womb led to...

> *"suffocating and extinguishing it"*

Which in turn, prevented conception. Of course, avoiding conception may have been the result of a lot of energetic jumping, sneezing, urinating, or any of a plethora of herbals, but Magnus was pretty sold on this one.

Chapter 11

Sex and How to Avoid It

Now all this is good and well for the Medieval woman who was interested in having sex either in a married or professional situation, but what of the woman who just really wasn't too keen? Did she have options? She absolutely did. A number of them, as it turns out.

Just Say No

We've talked about this in Chapter One. Pay attention. If you aren't that keen, for whatever reason, *Just Say No*. Make up an excuse if you have to, but stand your ground.

Secular Chastity

As mentioned in an earlier chapter, the reluctantly married woman who wanted to avoid her marriage debt might take a vow of chastity. It was a little unusual, but it wasn't unheard of. A declaration of burning devoutness did the trick. Yes. A sudden love of Christ and a vow of chastity and she was completely off the hook. Even the church could not criticize the ardent love of God as a reason to not get naked with the man you married.

Hallelujah, I'm convinced, it's chastity for me!

A chaste life had the fantastic advantage of not only avoiding the marital obligations, but keeping the lifestyle of a worldly and often rich woman. Court appearances, travel to exotic lands under the guise of pilgrimage, fine clothing, expensive jewellery, and a higher standard of food: none of that had to be forsaken. Just the sex. What a shame.

Of course, there are countless instances of genuine vows of chastity taken both inside and outside of marriage. One can only imagine how it would have gone down on social media if Facebook had have been a thing in the fourteenth century:

Maud and John have just gotten married and are on Facebook updating their statuses.

John updates status to Just Married.

Maud updates status to Just Married.

Maud: *Hey everyone! Great wedding and thanks for the gifts! John and I would like to extend our heartfelt gratitude to everyone who witnessed the marriage! I'd just like to let you all know I'm so thankful to my parents for arranging such a great husband that I'm taking a vow of chastity and will remain pure and devote myself to prayer for the rest of my marriage. I'm that thankful!*

Maud updates status to In a Relationship with God.

Agnes likes this.

Margery likes this. Lol.

Alice likes this. Wahahahahhahahaha nice one!

Brother Burchard likes this.

Robert puts a sad face emoji.

Charles: *Wtf, John. What just happened?*

John updates status to It's Complicated.

Margaret likes this.

Alice likes this.

Eleanor likes this.

John just checked in to The Maidenhead, London.

And quite frankly, who could blame him? Being married and being chaste wasn't for everyone.

Margery Kempe of Lynne

Around 1413, an Englishwoman named Margery Kempe negotiated a vow of chastity with her husband which, quite frankly, probably came as a bit of a relief to him. Let me explain.

Much has been written about the extraordinary life of Margery. She was born in 1373 to a world of mixed emotions about women. Some women were doing well, running businesses, but others were taking the more traditional role of stay-at-home wife and mother. It appears that Margery thought she might like to do both. She was mostly illiterate herself, but published her autobiography, *The Book of Margery Kempe*, in English by getting a helpful scribe to write it for her whilst she dictated.

Margery lived in Lynne and was the mother of fourteen children. Fourteen! She, like many other wives, ran a brewery and a horse mill and unlike many other wives, travelled extensively. Margery was extremely and genuinely devout, continually weeping and wailing and fainting, frequently overcome with spiritual emotion brought about by her love of her heavenly father, much to the annoyance of her travelling companions. All this with fourteen children who don't appear to have gone with her on pilgrimage.

All things considered, I would have thought surely she wouldn't have too much trouble convincing her husband to respect her vow. He was not for it, the story goes. Maybe he thought the hysteria and weeping would stop with some good loving.

Religious Chastity

Genuinely devout women could take the veil and opt for a life of religious contemplation in an actual religious institution. These women fell into two categories; those who were virgins who entered the religious life and remained virgins and those who took up a religious vocation towards the end of their life and abstained from sexual relations and the temptations of the outside world afterwards.

Both had their unique set of challenges. The virgin often longed for a life she had never known, and the later-in-life converted vowess may miss the life she had known and find she really didn't like being without it.

Late Converts

There might be a number or reasons for taking the veil later in life, but the number one reason was the overwhelming fear of actually spending eternity in hell as punishment for a life of luxury, excesses, pleasures of the world, and carnal desires. Hell was not a vague threat. It was a real physical place as far as the Medieval woman was concerned, and spending any amount of time there was to be given some serious thinking about. Purgatory didn't sound like a lot of fun either, but at least there was hope of redemption through the prayerful intervention of others who were still living, even if the recently departed had to pay for them herself. As women aged and the hour of death approached faster and faster, atonement was not only necessary to get to heaven, but extremely vital.

How could she make this happen?

Ellen of Udine

One such repentant woman is the Blessed Ellen of Udine. After a fabulous life in the broader community, Ellen's husband passed away, leaving her with sombre thoughts of not only where he was spending eternity, but also her own future. She took numerous steps to save her soul, which was the highly recommended path to take. She gave generous donations to charities, which the church approved of. She gave generously to chantries for the saying of prayers for her soul after she had died, which the church approved of. She adopted the strict lifestyle of a penitent of the church, which the church approved of. She whipped herself regularly to purge her earthy body and wore abrasive clothing and stones in her shoes, which was also seen as a good move.

Ellen took it up a level by taking a vow of silence—which was not strictly necessary—but not before she had made her confession:

> *I wear a hair shirt because of the silken undergarments… with which I used to clothe myself. Thirty-three stones I put in…my shoes because I have so often offended God with my leaping and dancing. I flagellate my body for the impious and carnal pleasures with which I indulged it during my marriage.*

Her efforts to suffer and emulate the pains suffered by her Lord were typical of the genuinely sorry woman who felt she had a great deal to make up for. As long as one didn't have a penchant for whippings, this was approved by the church, too.

Ellen must have taken part in some quality sinning and excesses to feel that this kind of atonement was completely necessary. Silken underwear instead of linen does sound like it is an excess, but it's hardly whipping-yourself-in-a-repentant-frenzy kind of an excess. Perhaps she should have been a better human being all along and just settled for some quality time on her knees in thoughtful, reverent prayer instead. Stones in one's shoes are guaranteed to ruin the leather, and that's just a wasteful misuse of resources. Another round of flagellations for you, Ellen.

Whilst this kind of dramatic action was admirable on all fronts, many women who were cloistered together for long periods of time without sex were, according to both doctors and their religious counterparts, setting themselves up for emotional problems as well, which might only be cured by exorcism. Exorcism. Okay then.

Jeanne Potier of Cambria

The church's worst fears came true in 1491 when there was a mass outbreak of this very kind of sex-hysteria at a Cambria convent. According to the records kept there, the undersexed Jeanne Potier started it when the stress of her enforced chastity

took a turn for the worse. She became a *hysterical nymphomaniac*, in the words of those who knew, and was promptly removed from the rest of the women. For the good of the greater community, she wasn't returned until her demons were exorcised and she became her old self again. A bit less communion wine and a bit more outdoors working in the sunshine for Jeanne, maybe.

Religious Chastity...Just Kidding!

Wealthy widows who were targets for remarriage might enter a convent under the guise of repentance and continue to live a fairly secular life with little or no religious contemplation, which was a recipe for disaster. Spending the rest of one's life with a bunch of religious people is not so bad if you're one of them, but could be extremely tedious for a person with no real desire to fast, pray, or live without men.

You'd imagine that religious houses would feel that this kind of woman was not especially welcome into their secluded houses of Godly contemplation, but it must be remembered that these women were often very wealthy and made charitable donations and bequests to the places they wished to stay, which made them quite lucrative recruits.

If that didn't really appeal, a lady might not join a nunnery, but choose to enter its restricted inner areas and just live really, really close.

Elizabeth de Burgh of Clare

Elizabeth started her life as a reasonably privileged young woman with wealthy, titled parents. She married well twice, wanted for nothing, and led a wonderful life, well-appointed with all the things a lady of her rank and social standing might acquire. She was a generous patron to artisans and religious houses alike.

Towards the end of her life, Elizabeth's thoughts turned to her future and the question of her everlasting soul. In 1342, she took

a vow of chastity and received a special indulgence from the Pope to enter the precincts of a religious house without becoming a nun. She had permission to take three ladies with her.

A little later on, the *three ladies* was expanded to encompass *four or five honest women* and *three honest and mature men*. Not long after that, Elizabeth was allowed to stay overnight with the nuns in the Minoress's area. In this way, she did not have to give up her secular life to partake of the religious one, also. She had to remain chaste and sexless, though, so the choice to allow three men to live in the precinct with her is interesting.

Even more interesting were the young women with absolutely no religious calling who were often deposited in religious houses as a safe holding ground to guard their virtue or as an educational opportunity until a suitable husband could be found. A nunnery was also a great place for men to stash away their unwanted lovers who were becoming tiresome or problematic.

The twelfth-century French scholar and philosopher Pierre Abelard did exactly that with his lover, who then became his wife. Initially, she had absolutely no religious vocation, but over the years became the abbess. An abbess with no real vocation and a desire to relive her carnal days with her lover, it must be said. This is her story.

Heloise d'Argenteuil of Paris

Heloise was born in Paris in 1101, and by the time she was a young lady, she was a ward in the care of an uncle, Fulbert, who was a canon in Paris. She was intelligent and already known far and wide for her studies before her uncle thoughtfully hired for her, a tutor.

Rather less thoughtfully, it was the very famous intellectual, Pierre—or Peter, as he is known in English—Abelard. Pierre was much her senior in years and a well renowned teacher. After moving into the house where Heloise lived, Pierre seduced her,

and they spent more time engaging in carnal sins than looking at books.

Not so surprisingly, Heloise became pregnant and was promptly whisked off to Pierre's sister's house to have their baby. Needless to say, when Uncle Fulbert found out, he insisted that they marry so Heloise wasn't shamed. Pierre agreed, as long as the marriage was kept quiet. Educational and promotional opportunities were better if he was unwed. What a guy.

In a move that shocked everyone, Heloise declared that she wasn't too keen on the marriage because love should be freely given and not owed in the bonds of matrimony. She agreed to wed eventually, much against her better judgement. Shortly after their return to Paris, Pierre decided it might be best for everyone if he installed Heloise in the convent of Argenteuil for the time being.

This went down rather badly with Uncle Fulbert and his friends. They felt that by making her a nun against her will, Pierre had essentially gotten rid of her. Retribution came swiftly when a group of men broke into the new groom's room one night and castrated him.

Filled with shame, Pierre became a monk in the Abbey of St Denis in Paris. Heloise eventually became prioress at the convent at Argentuil where she was still located against her will and any real vocational calling. Over the following years, Heloise and Pierre wrote letters to each other through which he sent his fraternal, holy love to her, and she sent her burning, earthly desire to him. Heloise never did gain a genuine calling for the religious life, even though she became Abbess at the Oratory of the Paraclete many years later and was buried there.

Problem Nuns

Church records of convent visits were constantly complaining about the women who lived there with no religious vocation who were dressing and eating like regular women and entertaining guests, some of whom may or may not have been men, in their cells. Okay, they were men.

Besides that, there was always the problem of women who had taken a vow early in life, thinking it was a serene way to avoid the outside world or an unwished-for marriage, but who, once actually living the life of a fully professed nun, found it not quite to their liking. Or not to their liking at all. Problems were bound to arise, and it seems that Alice Boyton was a repeat offender.

Secular woman with candle for Candlemas.

Psalter, with added Office of the Dead and litany, Walters Ex Libris. Manuscript W.35 folio 1v.

Alice Boyton of Salisbury

We don't know how old Alice was or why she took the veil in the first place, but we do know that she wanted out and clearly was indulging in un-nun-like activities. She was passed from abbey to abbey for her bad behaviour. A mandate from the bishop's register in Salisbury was getting sick of her wayward ways and was putting its foot right down:

> *1414. Mandate to the Prioress and convent of Bromhill to receive Alice Boyton, nun of Kensington St Michael, who is to be transferred on account of her bad behaviour. She is to be in the special custody of a mature, God-fearing nun and is to be kept from communication with secular or religious people except in the presence of this guardian. She is not to go outside the monastery until further notice. The house will be paid for her stay by the priory of Kingston St Michael.*

How do you solve a problem like Alice? Just keep passing her around and hoping for the best. A chaperone was also a good idea, but make it a chaperone who was unlikely to join her on her escapades, which may or may not have been a problem at one point, since it was apparently quite necessary to spell it out in the order.

The Widow Felmersham of Godstow Abbey

Visiting clergy were appalled at the kind of disruption to a life of prayerful and devout contemplation taking in women who did not have a genuine religious calling entailed. In 1434, Godstow Abbey found itself issuing some tough love after one of the widows repeatedly disrupted the tranquillity. On more than one occasion, it appears. From the orders that followed, it looks like the abbey was a little on the relaxed side before Felmersham got there, but that the widow ruined it for everyone.

> *Also that Felmersham's widow with her entire household and other mature women be removed entirely from the monastery within the coming year since they are disturbing for the nuns and the occasion of bad example by reason of their dress and their visitors.*

Even after the visitors and the dresses and the disturbing was pulled in check, there was further complaining by someone who was obviously not being invited:

> *Also that there be no parties and drinks after compline, but when it is over, all the nuns go together to the dormitory and lie there the night...except for the infirm who then shall be lying in the infirmary.*

Worse than that was to come.

> *Also that the beds in the nun's lodgings be entirely removed from their rooms other than those for the children, and*

that no nun receive secular for any recreation in their rooms under threat of excommunication. For the scholars of Oxford say that they can have whatever entertainment with the nuns they wish to desire.

Questions about why there were beds in the nun's quarters for guests in the first place might have been asked. It's quite admirable that the widow Felmersham brought her entire household with her to the monastery. One in, all in! And without a doubt, she needed nice dresses if she's going to be throwing parties and hosting drinks after compline. Of. Course.

That place must have been rocking! Except for the nuns. No party for you...off to the dorm. No wonder they complained. Student parties are the best.

Huguette du Hamel of Port-Royal

This advice on moral etiquette was completely ignored by one Huguette du Hamel, who was the abbess at Port-Royal in France. She was an absolute beacon to everything a nun should avoid as far as chastity was concerned. She kept a lover, Baudes le Maitre, and instead of instilling virtue in her younger nuns, actively attempted to include them in activities best described as wanton, like group bathing.

When those in charge got wind of what was going down in the abbey, they confronted Huguette, unceremoniously forcing her to give up her position and abdicate. Huguette took this news as well as might be expected. She immediately made off with the most of the abbey's valuable possessions and fled with her lover into the great unknown.

Margaret Wavere of Catesby

Meanwhile in England, the prioress of Catesby, a certain Margaret Wavere, was being held accountable for her own un-Christian behaviour. Like Huguette, she also had a lover, one William Taylour who was also busy setting a bad example and

not keeping his vows as a priest. His frequent visits did not escape the notice of others. Not entirely content to behave in an unchaste manner, Margaret added to her own personal finances by selling the silver service which belonged to the priory. No value is given for the silver, but you can bet that it wasn't the cheap set from the market. It would have been the top shelf one from the swankiest silversmith in the city.

Chastity After Death

Chastity after the death of a husband could take a few different forms, as we know. Entering a convent was a great option for the woman who wished to remain sexless and not remarry, and it went hand in hand with not affecting her current lifestyle too much if she chose.

A woman who lived in a busy town or a city, however, may well have had a trade which she loved and was in no hurry to give up. She may have worked alongside her husband and had as many skills as he did. After the death of a spouse in those circumstances, it was quite the usual thing to remarry to keep the business going. A woman might be permitted to work as a femme solo, hire and train apprentices, or according to guild regulations, only keep her business as long as she married a man of the same trade within a certain period of time.

One can see how theoretically this was a good idea. The goods aren't sold off, the premises don't need to be re-purposed, and the widow can continue her trade. She only needed the husband by her side to change from a deceased one to a new, living one. Perhaps a woman might *need* support to continue to run her husband's business. If she was not actively involved in the running of his work, she *would* need to marry someone suitable to keep the endeavour open.

On the surface, it allowed a widow to continue to make a living doing the trade she was competent in, and it ensured that any future husband was also skilled in the trade. Of course, if he was already skilled in the trade, the prospective husband might have been an ex-business rival whose interest was nothing more than getting his hands on the widow's workshop and assets. What was a woman to do? She could train and marry one of the apprentices, but if she were much older and he was quite young, this was likely to be unsatisfactory.

A funeral.

1470 Book of Hours of Flanders Jean de Wavrin. Walters Ex Libris. W267. Folio 86r.

At this point, there was only one way out for a widow who wanted to keep her business, work in it, and not be forced into a new sexual relationship. Surprisingly, this loophole comes from her departed husband himself.

Margaret Wod of York

Wills, like that of Thomas Wod's from York, dated 1494, stipulate that the wife inherits only if she doesn't have sex with anyone else.

> *Also I leave to Margaret my wife my terms in my fulling mill if she keeps herself sole after my death, if not then I will that my son William shall have them.*

It's quite possible that the son of Thomas was working alongside his mother and father in the fulling mill, and this was an active attempt to stop him from taking charge and ousting his mother.

Either way, Margaret was probably quite happy to stay single and keep her job.

Another man involved in the cloth trade felt very much the same way about his wife and his assets after he passed on.

Isabel Nonhouse of York

Another weaver named John Nonhouse, also from York, leaves items of his trade to his wife only under the same certain conditions. His will from 1440 is quite clear about the conditions. Whilst she remains single and therefore chaste, she inherits his business things. Should this change, then the two other men named get the goods:

> *And I leave to my son, Robert my best loom with all manner of tools in the house pertaining to my work. And I leave to William Whitwell one other loom with two combs always provided that Isabel my wife has the said two looms with all the tools pertaining to them whilst sole.*

Keeping herself *sole* meant keeping herself single, and it was implied that this also meant sexually continent.

Many modern women have been extremely angry about wills like this. They feel that the husband was overly jealous, manipulative, and wished to continue to control his wife's sexuality from beyond the grave. They are exceptionally angry that as a legal document, it could be upheld and the poor woman would be forced into perpetual chastity whether she wanted it or not or lose all her possessions if she didn't comply with his express wishes. There's a certain amount of truth to this, but there's a whole other side to it, too.

Take a moment and consider this: Suppose that the husband and wife loved each other, had built their business together, and worked side by side in it for years. Perhaps they had a couple of very able-bodied apprentices, and the wife was quite skilled herself. In the case of a woman who was capable enough

to run the business without him, what reason was there for her to remarry at all? Only social or guild-related reasons, and depending on the guild, they could be side-skirted.

Instead of reading wills like this as an effort to control a wife's sex life after her husband was no longer able to do it in person, perhaps the original intent was to give the grieving wife a way of continuing to run their business *by herself* with her apprentices under a perfectly legitimate umbrella of his express wishes.

A newly-widowed woman with a thriving business was a target for many men unless a husband specifically stipulated on his deathbed that there were terms and conditions to her keeping the business. His wife was unable to remarry. She must remain chaste. If not these things, then the goods and chattels were to be forfeited. This actually made her less of an attractive potential wife as well. Why should a man rush to marry her for her assets if she forfeited them by marriage? He would then be marrying only for love.

As a new widow, a woman is most probably not looking for love. Given the option to stay single and sexless and run her own business without a husband and still remain respectable? She might actually be quite okay with that, too.

Managing Chastity and Health

The health risks of being chaste was a delicate business when we know for certain that the humours needed to be considered. After all, a cold woman had her health to look after and it couldn't be ignored. She might die.

How was this to be countered? Were there options for these single, sexless women in convents or single women who had taken vows? They were supposedly not having sex. Some most definitely were, secretly, but what of the lady who genuinely wasn't? What then?

You know who we're going to seek advice from, don't you? Indeed. We can always count on Trotula to have something informative to say, and she does:

> *There are some women to whom carnal intercourse is not permitted, sometimes because they are bound by a vow, sometimes because they are bound by religion, sometimes because they are widows, because to some women it is not permitted to take fruitful vows. These women, when they have a desire to copulate and do not do so, incur grave illness. For such women, therefore, let there be made this remedy. Take some cotton and some musk or pennyroyal and anoint it and put it inside the vagina.*

If you're out of musk or pennyroyal, there's still hope for you yet. She continues:

> *And if you do not have such an oil, take trifera magna and dissolve it in a little warm wine, and with cotton or damp wool place it in the vagina. This both dissipates the desire and dulls the pain. Note that a pessary ought not be made lest the womb be damaged, for the mouth of the womb is joined to the vagina, like the lips to the mouth, unless, of course, conception occurs, for then the womb withdraws.*

Trifera magna appears enticingly in several of the Trotula recipes for women's complaints, but she doesn't actually state what it is or where to get it, whether to cook it or pulverise it. If it is completely unobtainable, just leave it out and use the wine. Apparently, you're likely to have wine hanging around the house if you're not getting any or just unlucky in love. That sounds about right.

Other doctors, like John Gaddesden from the Oxford University Faculty of Medicine in the fourteenth century, also advised that a woman who remained chaste, although admired for her purity and devotion to God, needed action. If, in this circumstance, a woman felt her health was at risk, she could seek a female doctor who was advised to assist medically to avoid the womb suffocating altogether. He wrote:

> *If the suffocation comes from the retention of the [female] sperm, the woman should get together with and draw up a marriage contract with some man. If she does not or cannot do this, because she is a nun and it is forbidden by her monastic vow or because she is married to an old man incapable of giving her her due, she should travel overseas, take frequent exercise and use medicine which will dry up the sperm. If she has a fainting fit, the midwife should insert a finger covered with oil of lily, laurel or spikenard into her womb and move it vigorously about.*

For medicinal purposes. Of course.

Which may have led to further confession-booth situations about possible lady-on-lady things which we mentioned right at the start. It's not too bad, as far as remedies go. Feeling a bit lustful? Overseas travel and some brisk exercise for you. Maybe take that midwife with you and make a weekend of it.

Chapter 12

When There's an Itch to Scratch

Sexually Transmitted Diseases

The modern world didn't invent sexually transmitted diseases. They've been with us as a people for a very, very long time. It was extremely unfortunate that there was very little medicine available to treat sexually transmissible infections, and the woman who encountered a man who had had many previous lovers was at a high risk of becoming infected with something herself. Gonorrhoea was well known. Syphilis came in towards the end of the medieval period. Many health manuals address the issues of venereal diseases as well as rashes, itching, lice, scabies, vaginal discharge, plague, and leprosy, some of which we know today aren't sexually transmitted diseases proper.

Doing his bit for sharing the love in a literal way was the fourteenth-century first duke of Lancaster, John of Gaunt. It was alleged, and no one likes to point the finger at a duke, that he...

> *...died of putrefaction of his genitals and body, caused by the frequenting of women, for he was a great fornicator.*

How do we know? A doctor of theology and Vice Chancellor of Oxford University, Thomas Gascoigne, who was born in 1404, accused him in a manuscript tucked away in the Lincoln College at Oxford.

It's quite easy for a woman to say no to an offer of sexual coupling to a regular man, but in the case of a titled nobleman, a refusal may offend more than a life was worth. If one was a prostitute, she had no choice whatsoever, and once infected, could expect to lose her job. Bleak news all round. Usually.

Jacote de Chateauvillain of Dijon

In 1436, Jacote appeared before the courts in Dijon for a sexual complaint which essentially involved her telling lies. What happened is this: She found herself in an attempted rape situation where her assailant was getting pretty insistent. Not surprisingly, but a little disappointingly, he was a priest. When she reported the attack and they asked how she had managed to fend him off, she replied that she had falsely told him that she was infected with *le gros mal*, the great evil, which may or may not have been any one of a host of venereal diseases: leprosy, pox, or the plague. The priest had been repulsed and figured she wasn't worth the risk, but it was pretty quick thinking on her part and it certainly did the trick. A round of cheers for Jacote, if you would, please.

Ladies who were rash in their sexual choices, pun intended, could suffer the consequences in the form of rashes, pustules, leprosy, or invisible, but still highly transmissible, infections. Leprosy was a term used for variable scaly skin complaints including psoriasis, scabies, and actual leprosy.

Itches and Rashes

Nothing is more unpleasant than an itchy rash on the nether regions. Obviously, there were methods to deal with such a small complaint, but what might they be? Let's refer to our favourite lady medic, Trotula, again. Where would we be without her?

She has advice for the secret lady part that itches for whatever reason:

> *If there is itching of the vagina, take camphor, litharge, laurel berry, and egg white, and let a pessary or enema be made. Galen says that a powder of fenugreek with goose tallow is good for the hardness of the womb, just as Hippocrates attests.*

Itches? Has just been given a sexually transmitted rash by her incontinent husband, more like it. And she, a virgin on her wedding night! Double standard, much?

Unlike other medications, Trotula felt the need to employ some quality name-dropping in case the remedy didn't work. If it went well, great! If it failed and didn't work, blame Galen or Hippocrates. Not her. It needs to be said that Trotula is quite fond of camphor in her medical prescriptions, so at the very least, even if they failed, the aroma must have been an improvement.

It's a bit concerning where she offers the advice for a pessary *or* enema. I'm not sure exactly how an enema is helpful to the itchy front bit. It would need to be a really widespread patch of disgustingness before inserting medicine into the anus is likely to help. The reasoning is mystifying.

Other diseases that spread via close contact with others are inflictions such as scrofula, ringworm, scabies, ulcers, and abscesses. French villagers from Montaillou attempted to treat all of these at the sulphur baths at Ax-les-Thermes which may have had a certain amount of topical relief from some of them. A trip out of town to the spa certainly couldn't hurt, right?

Pustules

If itching isn't uncomfortable enough, perhaps the unhappy woman may be inflicted with pimples on her private parts. Herpes simplex is first recorded with the ancient Greeks and may have been out and about during Medieval times as well. It wasn't called herpes, of course, but watery pustules which match the description of herpes are recorded.

Thankfully, Trotula also handed down a remedy which she described as *decent* for the treatment of pustules in one's privates which was shared to other medical treatises. She gave no clues as to whether she meant this was a decent recipe or that it had

a decent chance of success. Either way, it's decent enough to try. What had a woman got to lose?

You'll be needing frankincense for this one.

> *Sometimes there arises pustules which turn into a very large lesion. Hence we should anoint these parts with an unguent which is good against burns caused by fire or hot water, and for excoriations of this kind.*
>
> *Take one apple, Armenian bole, mastic, frankincense, oil, warm wine, wax and tallow, and prepare them thus. We should place the apple, cleaned of both the exterior and interior rind and ground, on the fire in a pot with the oil, wax and tallow; and when they have boiled, we put in the mastic and frankincense, both of which have been powdered. Afterward, it should be strained through a cloth. Note that if anyone because of any burn has been anointed with this ointment, on the anointed place there ought to be a leaf of ivy cooked in wine or vinegar, or a leaf of gladden. This remedy is decent.*

It sure is something.

Apart from trying to discover what mastic actually is, a woman also needs to go to the trouble of acquiring Armenian bole, not the regular kind, with no clues to what either of them are. One was expected to just know these things. What bole was. What Armenian bole was. Where to buy it. Might one find it at a green-grocers or at the fish market? Any clue at all would be appreciated. Trotula was unhelpful about acquisitions for her recipes, to say the least.

Armenian bole, as it turns out, is an earthy clay from Armenia. No, really. It's high in iron oxide which gives it a distinct red colour, and also contains silicates of aluminium and quite possibly magnesium. Mastic is slightly less alarming, being a natural resin produced by the mastic tree. It's usually known by its common name of gum in Arabic.

Lice

Lice, of course, was an ongoing concern to Medieval people generally, not just women, so pubic lice may have been sexually transmitted or simply caught from bedding, since sleeping naked was the usual thing to do.

Guillemette Benete of Montaillou and Alazaís Rives of Montaillou

Many of the records from the village of Montaillou in early fourteenth-century France describe grooming lice off one another an act which is neither hidden nor shameful. Lovers picked lice from the bodies of one another. Family members did. Husbands and wives felt no shame in picking lice off each other in full view of passers-by. Vuissane Testaniere was providing information about heretics in her village when as part of her conversation the transcriptions record her saying:

> *"At the time when the heretics dominated Montaillou, Guillemette Benete and Alazais Rives were being deloused in the sun by their daughters, Alaizaid Benet and Raymonde Rives. All four of them were on the roof of their houses. I was passing by and heard them talking."*

Delousing was a job carried out by women, usually who had some kind of relationship with each other. The shame we associate with lice these days was entirely lacking.

Unlike other towns and cities, the inhabitants of Montaillou bathed infrequently, focussing on the parts of the body which could be seen and were used: the hands and the face. Many other women in many other parts of the country were a little more circumspect with regard to personal hygiene and the lice situation and wanted remedies to help kill the lice rather than just rely on the manual removal of them.

The English translation of Trotula's compendium of helpful recommendations gives us two recipes for the treatment of body and pubic lice.

> *For lice which arises in the pubic area and armpits, we mix ashes with oil and anoint.*

As any good Medievalist knows, a combination of ashes and fat makes an incredibly great soap, so in this respect, a soap-like compound seems like it would work. Soap is definitely worth trying if a person has lice, pubic or otherwise.

She gives another treatment for the ridding of lice which is specifically around the eyes. If soap hadn't deterred them from your pubic area, it's certainly worth a shot. You'll need bacon for this one.

> *We should make an ointment suitable for expelling them... Take once ounce of aloe, one ounce of white lead and frankincense, and bacon as needed. Let it be prepared thus. We grind the bacon very finely and we place the remaining ingredients which have been powdered (in it).*

As a product for lice, it seems a little fancy. Frankincense again? Is that a product a regular woman is likely to have lying around her house? I fear not. The use of lead is more than a little alarming for the eye area and only slightly less so for the use on genitals. Significantly more disturbing is the potential waste of perfectly good bacon.

The Three Magi at The Stable. 1470.

Book of Hours of Jean de Wavrin, Flanders. Walters Ex Libris. W.267. folio65r.

That the three wise men thoughtfully brought the Virgin Mary some gold, frankincense, and myrrh to celebrate the birth of her child has always struck me as odd choices. Yes, they were expensive gifts, but not terribly useful, were they? I'd always felt that a hot dinner of some kind would have been a more practical present for the new mother, but perhaps they were a better post-birth care gift than meets the eye on the surface.

All is quiet at the manger. Mary is exhausted after a busy eve of birthing, the new babe is swaddled and tucked away in a manger. Sadly, there was no crib for a bed, but women are resourceful, and she had made do. Joseph was chatting with a bunch of shepherds who had just dropped by and looked to be staying for tea. Quietly, she wished they'd brought some of their much-lauded shepherd's pie, but no dice. Just as Mary begins to think that she'll be the one making dinner again tonight, more visitors arrive. Mary perks up. Perhaps they'd brought food.

Wise Man 1: *We are three wise men.*

Mary: *There are three of you, that's for sure.*

Wise Man 2: *We come to pay homage.*

Mary: *Not to cook dinner?*

Wise Man 3: *We come bearing gifts!*

Mary: *Gifts? Like a fruit basket? Cheese platter? Packet of mixed nuts?*

Wise Man 1: *(Uncertainly) We have travelled afar...*

Mary: *How far? Pizza and pasta far?*

Wise Man 2: *We have come from the Far East...*

Mary: *The far east? Dim sum and karaage chicken far?*

Wise Man 3: *Much better!*

Mary: *Curry! Yessss! You guys are the best!*

The three wise men shuffle their feet anxiously.

Wise Man 1: *I bring you gold! It's good if your stomach is cold and full of mucus.*

Mary: *What are you saying?*

Wise Man 2: *I bring you frankincense! It's great for pubic lice.*

Mary: *Now wait just a minute! How DARE you suggest...*

Wise Man 3: *I give you myrrh! It chases overflowing lust or desire from the body. Just streak it a little on your chest for best results.*

Mary: *I cannot believe what I am hearing. You three are unbelievable!*

The three wise men look awkwardly at each other.

Mary: *Not even a casserole between you?*

We've all been there. Men can be hopelessly clueless about presents.

Leprosy

In cases of leper sex, Medieval medicine had a few ideas for the woman who was inflicted. Technically, leprosy wasn't a sexually transmitted disease in that leprosy can be caught without sexual contact. We know that today, but during the Middle Ages, the thought was quite different. It was definitely seen as a result of a sexual liaison with an unclean woman. It was highly contagious, so in one sense, it was true. Sex with a leper was guaranteed to end badly for the person having it.

Lepers were also credited with being especially lusty, which was unfortunate, as on the whole, no one wanted to be lusty with them.

Woman Feeding a Leper in a Bed.
Ms. Ludwig VIII 3, fol. 43. 83.MK.94.43. Getty Images.

As early as the thirteenth century, medical texts assured women that they might be left unharmed after having intercourse with a leper. It was completely safe for her. The next sexual partner would contract it, instead.

The reasoning behind that exciting bit of news was that according to the four humours theory, the coldness of the female womb meant that the emissions of the leper would remain in the woman's uterus, where it would turn into toxic and contagious vapour. This in itself was not enough to make the woman sick. The next man who had sex and placed his penis into the vaporous vagina of the woman, however, was guaranteed to become infected. Sores would quickly materialise before spreading over his body leading to certain doom.

Arnaud de Verniolle's Prostitute of Montaillou

This was so much so the contemporary thought, that when Arnaud de Verniolle, a priest from the village of Montaillou, was a young man, he had a sexual tryst with a prostitute that caused him to break out in what he believed was leprosy. He said, later…

At the time they were burning the lepers, I was living in Toulouse; one day I did it with a prostitute. And after I had perpetrated this sin my face began to swell. I was terrified and thought I had caught leprosy; I thereupon swore that in future I would never sleep with a woman again.

The fact that the prostitute didn't appear to be leprous herself makes it seem more likely that he picked up something else entirely unrelated to his visit. A swelled face indicates mumps, perhaps. It certainly didn't stop him from sleeping with women or taking various lovers afterwards, but by his own admission, he was put off quite a bit for a whilst and began to abuse young boys instead. Try not to be surprised.

Men who were used to frequenting a brothel or prostitute often brought home diseases to their new brides when they married, leading to any number of perplexing gynaecological complaints about which not a great deal could be done. One might try some home remedies or pray really, really hard and hope for relief. Odo de Beaumont, prayed with a fervour to St Thomas a'Becket after he caught leprosy or something like it after a late-twelfth-century visit to a prostitute and was cured. It probably wasn't leprosy then.

Isolde of Ireland

Even in popular literature, the horrors of leper sex were present. The twelfth-century romance of Tristan and Isolde features a pair of accidental lovers who drank a potion and fell in love. The story goes that King Mark of Cornwall sends his cousin Tristan to fetch his beautiful new bride-to-be from Ireland. Her name was Isolde. During the trip home, Isolde and Tristan fall in love. Isolde goes on to marry King Mark anyway, and it all goes pear-shaped from there.

The lovers start a clandestine love affair, which is suspected and then eventually proved. And enraged King Mark is about to burn his wife, Isolde, for her crime of adultery when he suddenly decides that a fate worse than death is to be sent to a leper colony as a prostitute instead. The lepers are quite excited about his decision and promise King Mark that Isolde will suffer for her adultery and that she will be taken advantage of in horrible ways. They said:

> *Give us Isolde. She'll belong to all of us. Never did a lady know a worse fate. Lord, we have such ardent desires that there is not a lady on this earth who could more than a day stand to have relations with us. If you hand her to our lepers, then she will see our lowly brothels.*

Naturally, she is rescued by her lover, Tristan. In the real world, there was no rescuing, and sex with lepers at a leper colony was a punishment threat which was a literal death sentence.

Chapter 13

Girls on Girls

There were women who refused to fit neatly into the ideals of the strictly religious confines of what it meant to be a woman. A woman was supposed to love a man, and that was how it should be. On this, the church was most emphatic. Asking anyone who worked in that direction to double check, just to be sure, would make a person deeply regretful.

The church was—try not to be surprised—incredibly poisonous towards anyone, much less a woman, who preferred the company of other women and who took part in so-called diabolical acts. And lesbians were almost as diabolical as they came. A person could tell their diabolical deeds if a man wasn't directly involved or if it was something out of the ordinary.

Lesbians

Stories abound of women who were cloistered together forming unnatural bonds of special friendship. Their words, not mine. Same-sex couples were not recognised as having any special rights or even acknowledged that they were a couple. They were just two women who were friends. Very good friends. Let's not think about exactly how good. If we did think about how good a friendship they had, we were in danger of walking into territory where sinning was happening, and the less time spent thinking about it, the better.

Women kissing. Carrow Psalter. Walters Ex Libris. Manuscript W.34. folio 23r.

The main problem with lesbians, according to the church, was that they were involved with secret girly touching and led other women away from marriage and husbands. *Tsk tsk*, for shame. Canonists didn't really know what to do with them, and often just looked the other way and focused on more pressing matters, like whose cow was allowed to eat the grass on the verge between two properties and whether or not the bread was undersized.

In the thirteenth century, there were unhappy mumblings from the usual direction of the pulpit about what to do about these women, because it seemed that we couldn't just leave them alone in happy domesticity to live as God intended.

By the fourteenth century, the mumblings and veiled comments developed into full-blown angst. Women who loved women in any other way than a firm, platonic friendship were now viewed with hostility. Women were cautioned not to form strong friendships with other women, just in case an unnatural attachment might blossom. Sermons were needed. Finger-pointing happened. Name-calling became nastier and more frequent.

Punishments for a woman wanting to live quietly with her woman beloved were angrily handed down from the pulpit. In some rare cases, death occurred. It really was completely uncalled for.

Theodore Weighs In

In the very early stages of frowning at lesbians, persecution was comparatively mild and in line with most other chastisements for most other misdemeanours. The eighth century confessional, the *Penitential of Theodore*, gave a penance of fasting for three years for a woman who had had carnal knowledge with another woman.

> *If a woman practices vice with a woman, she shall do penance for three years. If she practices solitary vice, she shall do penance for the same period.*

In this respect, sinning with a close female friend carried the same punishment as sinning alone, which is a bit surprising. Normally solo activities were slightly less punishable offences than group ones. Fasting for penance was defined as fasting for all holy days, not every day of the week. Mind you, there was an extremely large number of holy days. Saint's days, which made up public holidays, numbered around sixty a year, a lot of time for reflection of sins.

Burchard Weighs In

By the time the eleventh century rolled around, Burchard of Worms was busy scribing away at his book of penitent questions for the confessional. Burchard of Worms, he of the one hundred and-ninety-four confessional sex questions and with whom we became friends in an earlier chapter, was extremely worried about what kind of things lesbians might be doing in the privacy of their own homes. He thoughtfully added questions in his penitential *Decretium*, just to make sure they weren't.

He encouraged the priest taking the confessions to be thorough in his enquiries. There, we find question 154. One translation reads:

> *Have you done what certain women are accustomed to do, that is, to make some sort of device or implement in the shape of the male member, of the size to match your desire, and you have fastened it to the area of your genitals or those of another with some form of fastenings and you have fornicated with other women or others have done with a similar instrument or another sort with you? If you have done this you shall do penance for five years on legitimate holy days.*

A second translation which is quite similar, but has bonus extras added onto it, is well worth repeating in its full version:

> *Have you done what certain women are wont to do, contriving a certain engine or mechanical device in the form of the male sexual organ, the dimensions being calculated to give you pleasure, and binding it to your own or another woman's pudenda, and have you thus committed fornication with other evilly disposed women or they, using the same or some other apparatus, with yourself?*

That's three years on bread and water on fast days only. Or four years. Or for a nun having a lesbian encounter in this manner, seven years. Seven. Years. I quite like the way that as an afterthought he thinks to enquire not just whether the lady has been on the receiving end of the sex toy, but also on the giving end. And that women are evil. I think that's worth mentioning, don't you? He sure did.

Burchard didn't just leave it there. He had further questions about what certain women are wont to do, namely sitting upon the aforesaid instrument or some other device of similar construction, thus committing fornication upon yourself in solitude? The penalty for using a sex aid by oneself carried a penance of an entire year, even if a lonely lady had no one to play with. He seemed to have given it quite a bit of thought. Possibly alone. At night.

The downside to questions like this is that although some women may have been actually taking their late-night sexy times into their own hands, as it were, many others may not have even thought to...until then. So, no, I hadn't, but what a fabulous idea, thanks! Any woman with slightly improper urgings may be encouraged to take that next step and explore them properly.

Upon hearing this for the first time, a new bride might feel the need to discuss this with a close, female friend.

> *Cecily and Margaret are chatting. Cecily seems a bit thoughtful about something since she's come home from church, and finally decides to get it off her chest.*

Cecily: *You won't believe what happened in church today! Brother Edward asked me if I had fashioned a penis and strapped it to someone and fornicated with it!*

Margaret: *O.M.G. How unbelievably rude!*

Cecily: *It's beyond rude! A penis with straps!*

Stunned silence.

Margaret: *...but...well...have you?*

Cecily: *Margaret! How could you ask such a thing!*

Margaret: *Only...the men are packing for a crusade and they leave next Tuesday.*

Cecily: *Yes. My Edward is going, too.*

Margaret: *And that last crusade went on for over ten years...*

Cecily: *Ten years! That's a long time. Gosh.*

Margaret: *It's a very, very long time. It certainly makes you think!*

Cecily: *It certainly does.*

Margaret coughs.

Margaret: *What kind of straps do you think he was talking about?*

Hincmar Weighs In

Another hundred years after the *Penitential of Theodore*, the ninth century Hincmar of Rheims, who was archbishop at the time, had a bit to say about women who had relationships with their special female significant others and went to pains to spell it out in detail for anyone who wasn't quite sure what was going on:

> *They do not put flesh to flesh in the sense of the genital organ of the one in the body of the other, since nature precludes this, but they do transform the use of the member in question into an unnatural one, in that they are reported*

> *to use certain instruments of diabolical operation to excite desire.*

That they used *certain instruments* we already know from the questions asked to unsuspecting women in the privacy of the church confessional regarding things which are shaped like the male member and have straps on. Hinemar seemed a little shy about mentioning dildos at all, let alone what to call them, and had to settle for *certain instrument of diabolical operation* which is a ripping phrase, really.

Sadly for him, Hinemar's admonishments didn't seem to make much impact on the lives of lesbians, and quite frankly, it was all downhill from there.

Gregory Weighs In

Later, in the 1230's, Pope Gregory IX put the Dominicans in charge of sorting out the unacceptable level of homosexuality he believed Germany was suffering from deeply. He felt quite strongly that the whole situation was absolutely abominable and was quite loud about it.

On a sliding scale of *Oh-I-do-wish-you-wouldn't* to *I-hope-you-burn-in-the-fiery-pits-of-hell*, it was clear where his sentiments lay. Lesbians were positively dread-inducing. He felt:

> *[homosexuals are] despised by the world, dreaded by the council of heaven...more unclean than animals, more vicious than anything alive.*

Lesbians? Vicious? Viciously defending their right to not have their sexual organs dictated to by a supposedly celibate clergyman, perhaps. Happily, although Pope Gregory was angry about the situation, he didn't write up many punishments himself. His successors would do that for him.

Bede Weighs In

The Venerable Bede was an English Benedictine monk who lived quietly at the monastery of St. Peter. His life predated both Gregory and Hinemar, so in a way he started it. He was still being quoted years later by churchmen everywhere who felt he had a lot of valid things to say. Bede had a lot on his mind, but he was more concerned with the bad behaviour of religious women, especially nuns, than women practicing same-sex relationships outside the walls of his heavenly domain. Especially nuns who made phallic devices and played with them. Bede's canon regarding this gave a rather severe seven-year penance. The same as many other ones gave for sodomy.

St Augustine Weighs In

St Augustine was a figure of authority in religious circles. His advice was taken quite seriously, and when he spoke, people listened. He was kind of a big deal. Obviously, St Augustine cared deeply for the spiritual and corporal well-being of his flock. This naturally included sheep of both genders. Whilst his lay brothers had a lot of their own issues in regards to chastity, he realised that large amounts of women living together without men to see to their healthful needs might form unnaturally strong and close ties. Intimate ties, maybe. They were weak, and therefore needed guiding.

His feelings were that whilst spiritual love for the lord and each other was admirable and proper and holy and good, nuns must take pains to avoid sharing carnal, physical love together. Purity was important to God. Chasteness was important to God. Temptation was to be avoided. Situations which made temptation available should also be avoided or treated with extreme care. Hell and purgatory were only a step away for poor choices in this matter.

Three female souls in Purgatory. Fifteenth century. Book of Hours. Walters Ex Libris. Manuscript W.168, folio 167r.

The bishop of Lincoln expressed his concerns when he visited his diocese in Lincoln itself. In 1521, Burnham Abbey was undergoing some improvements and renovations, and whilst the nuns who lived there were making the best of a bad situation, he felt that temptation was surely right around the corner. In his records of the visit, he was emphatic:

> *The nuns now sleep two to a bed until the dormitory is repaired and made ready. The bishop directed that from now on they do not lie together, but in separate beds.*

Sleeping together might lead to impurity, obviously, but there were other traps to dodge if a woman wished to avoid becoming tangled into a sinful situation. Bathing, for instance, was an activity which might lead to impurity, unchasteness, and the kind of love which he'd like to see avoided.

Obviously, cleanliness was next to Godliness, and the usual washing of face and hands in a basin of water should be encouraged as usual. Taking a trip to the baths might be temptation central, however. For this reason, St Augustine

recommended that holy women go to the baths only once a month. Even then, they should go there in groups of three or more, so instead of two soapy ladies in the tub, there might be more.

I'm not sure he was helping when he recommended that.

Matthew Weighs In

The Medieval chronicler Matthew Paris wasn't shy about being rude to uncloistered women. Perhaps he felt the nuns were adequately picked on and that someone, a man, perhaps, needed to turn their critical eye outwards into the broader community. He obviously saw himself fit for the job.

Matthew was quite familiar with the passages from the bible that alluded to lesbians, but appeared to have a very poor grasp of actual medicine. He tells an improbable story:

> *A good-looking noblewoman...impregnated another woman...and in some weird way became a father.*

The only thing really weird about that is that he thought it was not only plausible, but definitely true. Gullible is the word which I feel applies here. So. Very. Gullible. Matthew was also a huge fan of the bible, and in particular, Romans 1:26 which assured him that the women who took passive as well as active roles in the bedroom were rife with vile affections. He agreed:

> *Such people have a deservedly abhorrent and filthy reputation.*

Trash talk like that is unlikely to get a person invited to threesomes. I'm just saying.

Sex Toys

By now you've already come to understand that toys in the form of dildos for the lonely lady, or the lady who had a very special friend, were very much a Medieval thing. Forget fornicating with vegetables when a lady could have an actual penis fashioned to play with on those long, lonely nights. Or short nights. Or afternoons.

One assumes that since fake penises aren't considered coitus with an actual man, perhaps the rules of when and where sex can be had simply didn't apply here. Let's take a few minutes to revisit what we have learned about dildos in case someone has skipped ahead and missed a few chapters to get to the bit that interests them most. *Tsk tsk*. Naughty.

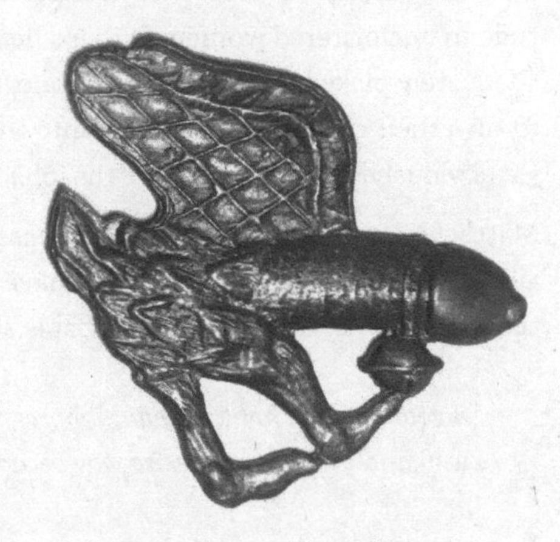

Winged Penis secular pewter badge. Reproduction of an original.

We know these things about dildos:

- They might have straps, all the better to play with a friend. Confessional advice.
- They might not have straps. All the better to play solo. More confessional advice.
- They are shown by the basket full. Marginalia manuscripts of naughty nuns.
- Several images show the cat running away with them. More manuscripts.

- They are fashioned in the shape of a man, presumably with testicles since pictures show this.
- In one case, a working model was made. It might go hard or soft.

We'll get to that one in a minute.

Lesbian Law

Medieval churches being what they were—that is, extremely lesbian-unfriendly—might a woman hope for a little more leniency in attitude from the civil courts? Perhaps? In some places, maybe, but absolutely not in thirteenth-century Orleans. The year 1270 saw a set of laws passed which stated that dismemberment was recommended for actual convicted lesbians. Should a third conviction be made by the same women, what was supposedly left of her after two previous dismemberments was to be burned alive.

To the best of my knowledge, the same court roles do not show any convictions or records of either of the punishments being carried out. Only one court case resulted in a penalty of death by drowning, and that was the unusual case of Katherina Hetzeldorfer in 1477.

Women Who Wanted to be Men

Nope. As far as the courts and the church were concerned, that was not cool. Not even maybe. There was no loophole, no if's, but's or maybe's. If you were born with the lady parts, you might be a lesbian, but you were still a *female* lesbian. Wanting to be a man was not okay. Just don't go there. But at least one woman did.

Katherina Hetzeldorfer of Speyer

The problem that the courts had with Katherina in 1477 was that she was a woman, which was bad to start with. She liked other women, which was very bad. She was also a woman who wanted to be a man, which was so very, *very* bad. She went so far as to dress and live her life as a man, which was so really, very, breathtakingly bad.

Katherina hadn't been born as an intersex person, so she had female genitalia *only*, which, according to the church and society, meant she had absolutely no right whatsoever to want to be a man. None! An intersex person might choose to be a woman or a man, but a woman with only the female bodily accoutrements was most certainly, as designated rather loudly from the pulpit, a person with no options whatsoever. No. Options.

Katherina brought a world of unhappiness upon herself by not even being content to be a lesbian and love other women the way other lesbians did, which was also a sin, but a less terrible sin than the ones she committed. The town of Speyer in Germany tried her for living and dressing as a man. She was in all appearance a man. She had a wife who was a woman, although apparently, there are no records to verify that an approved and legally binding marriage had taken place.

An examination of her wrongdoings included her fashioning of a male member out of leather, cotton, and wood. It was a rather exceptional piece, perfect for committing carnal offences with another woman, or *roguery* as it was called in this case. Whilst this seems like standard stuff we've seen alluded to before, the extremely talented Katherina's appendage was able to be used to urinate out of and lie erect when in use or flaccid when not in use.

Although married, during the trial, Katherina also was accused of whoring with prostitutes like a man.

The court room must have been positively agog with the amount of transgressions she had committed and had a hard time of it deciding which of the crimes was the worst and in what order the items needed to be dealt with. By and large, the absolute worst one was seen to be that Katherina rose above her birth gender and gave herself a higher male status, which was completely undeserved. The nerve of her!

Chapter 14

Dual Nature: Intersex Persons

Intersex Persons

There were people who didn't fit neatly into the ideals of the strictly religious confines of what it meant to be a woman or a man. This was the gender who fell—or were pushed—outside the society construct of the Middle Ages. In that world, they were regarded as abominations. We don't see them that way today, but it must be said that they were the Medieval church's least favourite people. We shall look at them together.

Hermaphrodites were what they called them.

Although it was a word used in medical and legal texts during the medieval period, we do not use it today. It is insulting and derogatory, and I will only use it here in direct quotes for the purpose of historical accuracy.

The attitudes of Medieval society expressed here are also in direct relation to the feelings of the time. Certainly, they are awful. A person who was born with both sets of functioning genitals was viewed in several different ways. Here, we take a look at the views of the intersex person in regard to the Medieval world. The views expressed here are of the Middle Ages and will quite rightly horrify a modern reader.

With our mixed Medieval emotions in heart and hand, let us ask, is there anything we know about these people possessing both sexes? Anything at all?

You had better believe we do, and not much of it is good. You aren't surprised even a little bit, are you?

Salmicis and Hermaphroditus the Greek

The term *hermaphrodite* comes from the Latin word *hermaphroditus*. Greek legends from Ovid tell of Hermaphroditus, the son of Hermes and the goddess of love, Aphrodite. He was a handsome young man who caught the eye of the nymph, Salmicis. Once smitten with a lot of loving feeling for him—and only him—she prayed to the gods in Olympus to be forever united with him. The gods felt pity for her and merged their two bodies into one, which probably wasn't what she had in mind at the time.

Aurora Consurgens; A Document Attributed to Thomas Aquinas on the Problem of Opposites in Alchemy. Commons.

This demonstrated the feeling amongst Greeks that a person who possessed both sets of genitals was not defective, but rather, a purposeful creation, one of God's beings.

As always, learned Medieval scholars had agreed that everything was the will of God, and therefore, his creations were each perfect and of his design. Things exist and unfold the way they do because they are part of his plan and because He wills it. This is particularly true of Medieval medicine. A remedy that is all but guaranteed to work will still only do so if it is the will of God.

Should the patient die, this was no failing of the herbs or the medicine or the surgery. It was because it was undoubtedly the will of God.

With this in mind, the Medieval world was gender inclusive, although a lot of time was spent arguing about it. Outside, what was seen as the two regular sexes co-existed with a third one which was both regarded as being perfect or damned, depending on who you asked.

This is where it got tricky. An intersex person, that is, a baby born naturally with both male and female sexual organs was viewed as a number of conflicting ideals. These ranged from either perfection, suspicion, revulsion, or as an abomination. They were hinted at and alluded to in tales, but usually not named, with the exception of medical texts.

Isidore Weighs In

Fast forward to the seventh century, and already the feeling was starting to change. No longer were intersex persons regarded as perfect and deliberate beings. They were less perfect and more monstrous, though still quite deliberate. Isidore of Seville was very careful not to offend God by calling them unnatural monsters because people were not familiar with them. Intersex people were still created by a divine will, although it was a bit confusing as to what that will was. In his eyes, they were God's monsters, which was a very fine line between being okay and not okay.

Others felt quite firmly that these people were abominations. Church people, I'm looking at you.

St Augustine Weighs In

Adult intersex people occasionally found themselves described despairingly in bestiaries. Augustine was also unkind enough to include them as monstrosities in his work, *The City of God*, which feels extremely uncharitable and not the least at all Godly. In

spite of this, some people steadfastly clung to the belief that all of God's children were God's children, purposefully created. How were they created, you may well ask? How, indeed.

Making Babies

From a medical point of view, it all stemmed from the initial pregnancy where the seed of the man fell into one of seven specific cells in the womb. Each cell was responsible for the attributes of the future baby leading to either a very feminine girl, a regular girl, a regular boy, a very masculine boy, and so on.

A child with both genders was formed when the sperm fell in the extreme middle cell. It was quite usual that in the cases of a middle-cell baby, the sex of the child was chosen by the parents when the child was an infant, and it was raised as either a girl or a boy. How intersex babies weren't killed at birth is a small mystery when infanticide rates were high amongst families who didn't get the offspring they hoped for. Baby girls were sometimes killed simply for being girls.

Should a child be brought up as a girl, there was only one opportunity to have her gender reassigned, and that was at the time of her marriage. Leaving an intersex child to live as both was not an option. In cases like this, one hopes the prospective groom knew what he was signing up for.

Medieval society being what it was, fussy about labelling everything so it could be in its proper place, was keenly interested in categorising intersex persons as either male or female.

Henry de Bracton Weighs In

In 1235, a treatise was written called *On the Laws and Customs of England* by Henry de Bracton which cleared things up for those who weren't sure about what was going on. He wrote that mankind is male, female, or *hermaphrodite*, but:

> *A hermaphrodite is classed with male or female according to the predominance of the sexual organs.*

Whilst that seems a little arbitrary, one can see what the idea behind his ideas were, although until puberty and the onset of breast tissue development, the only thing to go on as a baby is the lower organs which might be of equal size. Upon puberty, breasts would either develop and make a predominantly *female* intersex person, or the muscles and chest would develop and make a *male* intersex person. This is Medieval thinking. We don't do this now.

Henry of Segusio Weighs In

Not entirely happy with that definition, later that century another Henry, the canon lawyer Henry of Segusio in Italy, added that in the case of a perfect specimen, where neither sex prevailed, a sex should be chosen and adhered to under oath.

Hugh of Pisa Weighs In

Yet another thirteenth-century canon lawyer, Hugh of Pisa, suggested that other factors might help define the true gender of such a person. A beard, perhaps. Preferring the company of other men and the preference for manly activity was surely a sign of the dominant gender. This was true Medieval logic at its finest.

The Naked Bearded-Woman of Limerick and the Naked Man-Ox of Wicklow *(detail) in Topographia Hibernica, ca. 1196–1223, Gerald of Wales.*

The British Library, London, Royal 13 B. viii, fol. 19.

A person who chose to be female in this sense was expected to grow her hair long, wear female clothing and other female dress accessories like rings, girdles, and brooches, and keep herself chaste like other women did. She was also expected to marry

and give her husband his marriage debt. If she was unable or unwilling to do so, the union could be dissolved.

An illustration from an illuminated manuscript shows a naked woman with small breasts, muscular thighs, long hair, and a beard using a distaff. By the inclusion of the tools for women's work, we know that this person has chosen or been forced to choose the life of a woman and not a man. Men never spun wool with a distaff. In real life, the beard would have been shaven clean, but for the purposes of instruction, the person is shown with both attributes.

Peter the Chanter Weighs In

Further to dressing as a woman and taking the role of a woman, it was also expected that the person would only have sexual liaisons with men. Fornicating with other women, even if she had male equipment, was seen as quite definitely an abomination to mankind and God because it went against her freely-chosen gender. Peter the Chanter wrote about this in the twelfth century in his *De Vitio Sodomitico* and concluded that only one set of genital organs should be used for sex and that sodomy should be avoided, for that was what it was in the eyes of the legal system.

> *There will not be intercourse of men with men or women with women, but only of men and women and vice versa. For this reason, the church allows a hermaphrodite—that is—someone with the organs of both sexes, capable of either active or passive functions—to use the organ by which (s)he is most aroused or the one to which (s)he is more susceptible. If, however, (s)he should fail with one organ, the use of the other one can never be permitted, but (s)he must be perpetually celibate to avoid any similarity to the role of inversion of sodomy, which is detested by God.*

Peter the Chanter echoed the thoughts of other priests at the time. They weren't good ones.

The Dominican Case

One of the most interesting cases of an intersex person belongs to a woman in the early fourteenth century. The Dominican chronicle describes a woman who lived as a man's wife for ten years. It appeared that she had some anomaly with her vagina, and sex was not possible, though it's to be thought that it was at the very least attempted.

It appeared that she looked like a woman and had small breasts. After ten years, her husband appealed to the ecclesiastic courts, and the marriage was annulled. She was unable to pay him his marital debt and, even for a patient man, ten years is a long time.

After the marriage was annulled, the unfortunate woman sought the help of a surgeon who made an incision in her privy area. Astonishingly, a penis and testicles came out. Since she had not been able to function as a woman sexually, she was re-designated her gender as male. *He* then assumed the proper life of a man; worked in manual labour, got married to a woman, and was able to have complete proper carnal relations.

In this particular instance, the person was not seen as an abomination, merely someone who had been misdiagnosed at birth and to whom the correct organs had not made themselves known. Having been married as a woman and then again later as a man was not improper as the person, it seemed to the court, had been a man all along. They just didn't know it.

Appearing in Court

For the intersex person who identified as predominantly female, there was more bad news. In court cases where a witness might be required, Latin Canon and civil law in the *Decretum Gratiani* stated:

> *Whether a hermaphrodite may witness a testament, depends on which sex prevails.*

I can tell you right now which sex needed to prevail. Male. Male sex needed to prevail. This was the correct gender and allowed a person to take part in legal proceedings at that specific time. It was further spelt out in writing for those who couldn't read between the lines:

> *...as long as the sexual development was masculine enough to allow the person to be called male.*

Typical. Even with a penis, apparently a woman still wasn't good enough.

Eustace Deschamps Weighs In

The fourteenth-century French poet Eustache Deschamps had no great love or compassion for intersex persons who lived as either men or women and took the trouble to put pen to parchment and write a degrading poetic piece called *Contre les Hermaphrodites* describing their general lack of virtues, wrong body hair, and general unpleasantness. It's a *Ten Things I Hate About You*, only there are sixteen things crammed into even fewer lines.

> *A soft chin, son Hermaphrodite*
> *Effeminate, a defect of nature,*
> *Faint in heart, devoid of all virtues,*
> *But full of vice, which tends towards nothing but filth...*
> *A woman out of a man, who should be bearded,*
> *Man without hair, this is an insult to everyone.*
> *To meet them is nothing but misfortune,*
> *And their gaze can be pleasing to no one.*
> *They make sexual use of both kinds,*
> *I have known them in my time to be*
> *Untrustworthy, disloyal, evil.*

So, right up there with Eve in the Garden of Eden, then.

Unlike the many other causes and occupations that required heavenly intervention, there was no patron saint in the Medieval Catholic church for intersex persons. There is, however, a singular woman who was martyred in the fourteenth century and who is sometimes now associated with gender fluid people today.

This is St Wilgefortis.

Saint Wilgefortis

There is no question of whether she was a woman or not—she was female in the usual sense—but she was martyred for her abhorrent, manly features. You can tell it's her. She's the one on the cross wearing a dress and rocking a pretty luscious beard.

St Wilgefortis.

Book of Hours & Psalter, Sarum use. Latin MS 20. JRL1502655. Fifteenth century. John Rowlands Library. University of Manchester.

Around the mid-fourteenth century, Wilgeforce was extremely popular as the person to whom a woman might pray about an abusive husband. She was known by many different names, but is widely known by her English one of Uncumber.

In Westminster Abbey, there still stands a beautiful carving of her, wearing a long dress and holding a cross, fully bearded. It's in the Henry VII Chapel. In other depictions, she could be mistaken for Jesus on the cross, although the difference is that she has a dress, and he usually wears his usual loincloth. Now that we know what she looks like, who was she?

Wilgefortis of Portugual. Maybe.

The story goes that a young, beautiful noble woman named Wilgefortis had been promised by her father—who may or may not have been the King of Portugal, as is the usual thing with teenage women of means—in marriage. Her prospective groom was a Muslim king. He was wealthy, and her family were keen to make the alliance. Wilgefortis was a devout Christian, and the idea of marrying outside of her religion, and especially to a middle eastern man, was unacceptable to her.

In an effort to try and avoid the upcoming wedding, she took a vow of chastity which impressed no one, and prayed hard that she would be made repulsive to her intended. The story goes that God answered her desperate prayers in a manner most unexpected. She grew a luxurious beard.

As you'd suspect, the Muslim king was horrified and broke off the engagement the moment he saw her. Wilgefortis's father was so enraged, he had her crucified. Her own father! What a guy.

St Wilgefortis wasn't a lesbian, nor was she an intersex person, but she faced prejudice and an awful death at the hands of her father because she was no longer able to fulfil the role her society expected of her. She didn't fit neatly into a box, and there was no label for her.

For this, she was abhorred, treated as a freak, and killed.

Which sounds a little familiar, doesn't it?

Epilogue

As modern humans, we tend to project our ideals and belief systems onto people of the past, particularly women. We expect them to act the way we choose to act or to respond the way we would do in any given situation. In many cases, this is completely *not* how a Medieval person would behave, act, or think.

In the real world, a person who is an atheist shrugs their shoulders and says that they *never* would have behaved a certain way in a bygone era in history, but in actual fact, religion and the church had a very strong influence in the lives of these women, and if one was born into a time and place like the thirteenth or fourteenth centuries, you *did* care about your social standing and your good name in the community.

As we have seen, a woman could be outspoken and have strong opinions, but she needed to do it in a socially-approved manner. We all know that in many modern cultures today, the man is still seen as the head of the household, but we also all know that often it's his wife having the final say in a large number of domestic decisions. What's for dinner. Whether or not to buy that new car. The final say on which movie to watch that night.

It's going to be that chick flick that she's been *dying* to show you if you have any plans to get laid later in the evening, right? Happy wife, happy life, right?

Okay, so it's not always like that.

Most modern relationships are partnerships, with both parties having equal input into the decision-making. Some are still firmly entrenched in the old-school notions of He Is the Breadwinner and She Is the Homemaker. Others flip it, and the dad is the stay-at-home caregiver whilst the mother goes out to work. Sometimes, couples both do it all. Some women have relationships and others stay *femme solo* with cats.

These days, ours is a far more complex society, but in many ways, there are opportunities to live the way a person wants to live and be with whichever partner makes the heart race fastest.

The Medieval woman's sexual reproductive system was a relative prisoner to society, but there were women who lived outside of it, or women who just who took advantage of the legal loopholes offered to them. Taking a vow of chastity whilst still married to enjoy the finer things in life is the best example I know of.

Medieval women did the best they could. And who can ask for more than that?

Heartfelt Thanks

There are a number of people who really made this happen and to whom I feel a great debt of gratitude. I'd like to thank them, if I may.

Natasha Vera from Mango Publishing reached out about making the things I talk about into a book. It's something I'd thought about, but probably would never have actually done without her. Natasha, you're a champion. Tania from *Tania Crossingham's School of Illumination* created the artwork for the cover, the original of which is a treasured thing on my wall. I can't thank you enough. A huge thanks as always goes to Jenny, my long-suffering boss, who has given me the flexibility to do what I love doing, often on short notice. I would not be writing this without you.

Much love and thanks to friends and total strangers who turned up for the Between Linen Sheets: The Very Secret Sex Lives of Medieval Women presentations at a variety of odd locations and times. Your interest has been incredibly encouraging. Thanks to the Walters Ex Libris for making so many images available online and to the library staff at the BnF and the Hague who helped me through ordering images in a foreign language. Thanks, also, to modern people in the Medieval world who offered help and encouragement: Michelle Barton, Andrew McKinnon, Susanna Newstead, and my late-night cheer squad, Lauren Ball. A big thank you to Nigel Hendersen, who has a pickle.

Selected References

The Age of Adversity: The Fourteenth Century. Robert E Lerner. Cornell University Press. Ithaca, NY. 1968.

A Dictionary of Medieval Terms and Phrases. Christopher Coredon with Anne Williams. DS Brewer, Cambridge. 2004.

A History of Auricular Confession and Indulgences in the Latin Church. Charles Lea Hemy. Vol. 1. New York. Greenwood Press Publishers, 1968,

A History of Private Life. Revelations of the Medieval World. Phillipe Aries and Georges Duby, General Editors.

A Small Sound of the Trumpet. Women in Medieval Life. Margaret W. Labarge. Beacon Press, Boston. 1986.

Between Pit and Pedestal. Women in the Middle Ages. Marty Williams and Anne Echols. Markus Wiener Publishers, Princeton, New Jersey. 1994.

Book of Gomorrah. An eleventh century treatise against clerical homosexual practices. Peter Damian and Pierre J. Payer. Wilfrid Laurier University Press. Waterloo, Ontario, Canada. 1982.

But to Foule Lust and Likynge of Lecherye. Rachel Esa Scott. First taught at Atlantian University, #100. S.C.A. Kingdom of Atlantia. USA. 2 February 2019.

Chaucer's Canterbury Tales. For the Modern Reader. Geoffrey Chaucer. Prepared and Edited by Arthur Burrell, M.A. J.M. Dent and Co. London. May 1909.

The Close of the Middle Ages, 1273–1494. R. Lodge, MA, LLD, Prof History at Edinburgh University. Rivingtons. London. 1915.

Contraception: A History of Its Treatment by the Catholic Theologians and Canonists. John T. Noonan. Enlarged edition. Cambridge, Mass. Belknap Press of Harvard University Press. 1986.

The Corrector. Burchard of Worms in Ibid.

Culpeper's Complete Herbal & English Physician. Culpeper. Chrysalis Books. Greenwich Editions. 2003.

Dress in the Middle Ages. Francoise Piponnier and Perrine Mane. Translated by Caroline Beamish. Yale University Press. New Haven & London. 1997.

English Society in the Early Middle Ages. (1066–1307). Doris Mary Stenton. *The Pelican History of England.* Penguin Books. 1962.

Everyday Life in Medieval London: From the Anglo-Saxons to the Tudors. Toni Mount. Amberley Publishing. England. 2014.

Fashion in the Age of the Black Prince: A Study of the Years 1340–1365. Stella Mary Newton. Boydell & Brewer Ltd. The Boydell Press. 1980.

Female Sodomy: The Trial of Katherina Hetzeldorfer. 1477. Helmut Puff. Journal of Medieval and Early Modern Studies 30. 42 & 46. Winter, 2000.

From St. Francis to Dante, translations from the Chronicle of the Franciscan Salimbene (1221–88). G. G. Coulton, 2nd edition, revised and enlarged. 1907.

The Girdle of Chastity: A Medico-Historical Study. Eric J. Dingwall. Routledge. 1931.

Here Begins the Seeing of the Urines: an original 13th–15th Century Urine Diagnosis Pamphlet. Theophrastus von oberstockstall. The Restorers of Alchemical Manuscripts Society. 2014.

Hermaphroditism in the Western Middle Ages: Physicians, Lawyers and the Intersexed Person. Irina Metzler, Studies in Early Medicine I – Bodies of Knowledge: Cultural Interpretations of Illness and Medicine in Medieval Europe, BAR International Series 2170. 2010.

Hermaphrodites and the Medical Invention of Sex. Alice Domurat Dreger. Harvard University Press. Cambridge and London. 1998.

Hildegard von Bingen's Physica: The Complete English Translation of Her Classic Work on Health and Healing. Edited by Priscilla Throop. Healing Arts Press, 1998.

In Christianity, Social Tolerance, and Homosexuality: Gay People in Western Europe from the Beginning of the Christian Era to the Fourteenth Century. John Boswell. University of Chicago Press. Chicago and London. 1980.

Isidore of Seville. The Etymologies of Isidore of Seville. Edited and translated by Stephen A. Barney. Cambridge University Press. Cambridge. 2009.

The Lady in Medieval England 1000–1500. Peter Coss. A Sutton Publishing Book. Wren's Park Publishing. UK. 1998.

The Letters of Abelard and Heloise. Translated with an introduction by Betty Radice. Penguin Books. London. 1974.

Life in a Medieval Village. Francis and Joesph Gies. Harper Collins. 1991.

Life in Medieval France. Joan Evans. Phaidon. First published 1929.

Love Locked Out: A Survey of Love, Licence and Restriction in the Middle Ages. James Cleugh. Anthony Blond. London. 1963.

Making A Living in the Middle Ages. The People of Britain, 850–1520. Christopher Dyer. Yale University Press. 2009.

Making Sex: Body and Gender from the Greeks to Freud. Thomas Laqueur. Harvard University Press, Cambridge and London. 1990.

Meanings of Sex Difference in the Middle Ages: Medicine, Science, and Culture. Joan Cadden. Cambridge University Press. Cambridge and New York. 1995.

Medieval Cities: Their Origins and the Revival of Trade. Henri Pirenne. A Doubleday Anchor Book. Princeton University Press. 1925.

Medieval European Society, 1000–1450. Margaret Hastings. Douglass College. Random House. New York. 1971.

Medieval Fabrications. Dress, Textiles, Cloth Work & other Cultural Imaginings. Edited by E. Jane Burns. The New Middle Ages Series. Palgrave Macmillian. 2004.

Medieval Pets. Kathleen Walker-Meikle. Boydell & Brewster Ltd. The Boydell Press, Woodbridge, 2014.

Medieval Women. A Social History of Women in England 450–1500. Henrietta Leyser. Pheonix Giant Paperback. Orion Books. London.

Mistress, Maids and Men. Baronial Life in the Thirteenth Century. By Margaret Wade Labarge. Pheonix. Great Britain. 1965.

Montaillou. Cathars and Catholics In A French Village. 1294–1324. Emmanuel Le Roy Ladurie. Translated by Barbara Bray. Scholar Press. Penguin Books. England. 1978

On Sodomy. Peter Cantor.

On Union with God. Albert the Great. Ways of Mysticism Series. Continuum Publishing, Inc. 2000.

The Penitential of Finnian in Medieval Handbooks of Penance: A Translation of the principal libri penitentiales and selections from related documents. John T. McNeill and Helena M. Gamer, Eds. and Trans. New York: Colombia University Press, 1990.

The Penitential of Theodore. McNeill and Gamer.

The Regulation of Brothels in Later Medieval England. Ruth Mazo Karras. Signs Working Together in the Middle Ages: Perspective on Women's Communities 14, no. 2. 1996.

The Romance of the Rose. Guillame de Lorris and Jean de Meun. A new translation by Frances Horgan. Oxford World's Classics, Oxford University Press, 1994.

Sewers, Cesspits and Middens: A Survey of the Evidence for 2000 Years of Waste Disposal in York, U.K. Allan R. Hall and Harry K.

Kenward. Environmental Archaeology Unit. University of York. 1975–2003.

Sexuality in Medieval Europe: Doing unto Others. Ruth Mazo Karras. Third Edition. Routledge. London and New York. 2017.

Tacuinum Sanitatis. The Medieval Health Handbook. Translated and adapted by Oscar Ratti and Adele Westbrook. From the original Italian edition by Luisa Cogliati Arano. George Braziller. NY. 1976.

Terry Jones' Medieval Lives. Terry Jones and Alan Ereira. B.B.C. Books. 5 May 2005.

The Trotula: A Medieval Compendium of Women's Medicine. Edited and translated by Monica H. Green. Philadelphia: University of Pennsylvania Press, 2001.

The Western Medical Tradition: 800 BC to AD 1800. Lawrence I. Conrad. Cambridge University Press. 1995.

Transgressing the Boundaries of Holiness: Sexual Deviance in the Early Medieval Penitential Handbooks of Ireland, England and France 500–1000. Christine A. McCann, 2010. Theses 76.

Women in England, c.1275–1525: Documentary Sources. Edited by P.J.P. Goldberg. Translated by P.J.P. Goldberg. Manchester University Press. 20 November 2002.

Women and Gender in Medieval Europe. An Encyclopedia. Editors Mary Erler & Maryanne Kowaleski. University of Georgia. Georgia, USA. 1988.

Women, Family and Society in Medieval Europe. Historical Essays, 1978-1991. David Herlihy. Berghahn Books. USA. 1995.

Women in the Medieval English Countryside. Gender & Household in Brigstock Before the Plague. Judith M Bennett. Oxford University Press. New York. 1987

Women in the Middle Ages. The Lives of Real Women in a Vibrant Age of Transition. Frances and Joseph Gies. Harper & Row. New York. 1980.

Index of Women

About the Author

Rosalie Gilbert is passionate about living history, experimental archaeology, and women in the middle ages, particularly England, where her family origins are. She is a lifetime member of the Friends of the Abbey Museum of Art & Archaeology and a member of the Queensland Living History Federation.

Rosalie has been a guest speaker on Medieval Feminine Hygiene and The Very Secret Sex Lives of Medieval Women at The Abbey Museum of Art and Archaeology, for the Queensland Museum's *After Dark* Program, for the British Museum's *Medieval Power: Symbols & Splendour* Exhibition, the University of The Third Age's *Winterschool* Program, the *University Pavilion* at the Abbey Medieval Festival, and at various women's social groups.

Her hobbies include lying about being at work so she can stay home, hanging out with her rescue kitty, and eating nachos.

Mango Publishing, established in 2014, publishes an eclectic list of books by diverse authors—both new and established voices—on topics ranging from business, personal growth, women's empowerment, LGBTQ studies, health, and spirituality to history, popular culture, time management, decluttering, lifestyle, mental wellness, aging, and sustainable living. We were recently named 2019's #1 fastest growing independent publisher by *Publishers Weekly*. Our success is driven by our main goal, which is to publish high quality books that will entertain readers as well as make a positive difference in their lives.

Our readers are our most important resource; we value your input, suggestions, and ideas. We'd love to hear from you—after all, we are publishing books for you!

Please stay in touch with us and follow us at:

Facebook: Mango Publishing

Twitter: @MangoPublishing

Instagram: @MangoPublishing

LinkedIn: Mango Publishing

Pinterest: Mango Publishing

Sign up for our newsletter at mangopublishinggroup.com and receive a free book!

Join us on Mango's journey to reinvent publishing, one book at a time.

CPSIA information can be obtained
at www.ICGtesting.com
Printed in the USA
JSHW032320260323
39267JS00001B/1